WE TRAVEL AN APPOINTED WAY

A·W·TOZER

We Travel an Appointed Way

CHOSEN AND EDITED BY

HARRY VERPLOEGH

CHRISTIAN PUBLICATIONS

Camp Hill, Pennsylvania

Christian Publications
3825 Hartzdale Drive, Camp Hill, PA 17011

The mark of ⊕ vibrant faith

ISBN: 0-87509-407-4
LOC Catalog Card Number: 88-70130
© 1988 by Christian Publications
All rights reserved
Printed in the United States of America

Cover photo by Mike Saunier

CONTENTS

FOREWORD

We *Travel an Appointed Way* is the ninth volume in the collected editorials of A.W. Tozer. They were composed for *Alliance Life*, official magazine of The Christian and Missionary Alliance, during Tozer's 14-year tenure as its editor.

In the editorial chosen to head this collection, Tozer, like the reformer, Martin Luther, recognizes the fundamental human predicament to be unbelief. Only the man or woman whose object is the hidden God behind the Word of God possesses faith. "The person of true faith" believes that God orders each life despite the realities assessed by senses and intellect. He or she travels an "appointed way"—the journey ordered by the "secret script of God's hidden providence." It is a script in which misfortune is "outside the bounds of possibility."

The unbeliever cries, "I am God's pawn!" The believer sings, "I am God's beloved!"

May Tozer's readers, new and old, find spiritual nourishment in these eloquent distillations of Reformation faith.

The other volumes of editorials published to date:

The Root of the Righteous (1955)
Born after Midnight (1959)
Of God and Men (1960)
That Incredible Christian (1964)
Man, the Dwelling Place of God (1966)

God Tells the Man Who Cares (1970)
The Set of the Sail (1986)
The Next Chapter after the Last (1987)

Harry Verploegh
Wheaton, Illnois
April 1988

We Travel
an Appointed Way

To the child of god, there is no such thing as accident. He travels an appointed way. The path he treads was chosen for him when as yet he was not, when as yet he had existence only in the mind of God.

Accidents may indeed appear to befall him and misfortune stalk his way; but these evils will be so in appearance only and will seem evils only because we cannot read the secret script of God's hidden providence and so cannot discover the ends at which He aims.

When true faith enters, chance and mischance go out for good. They have no jurisdiction over them that are born of the Spirit, for such as these are sons of the new creation and special charges of the Most High God.

While sojourning here below, these children of the eternal covenant may pay token tribute to nature; sickness, old age and death may levy upon them, and to the undiscerning eye, they may seem to be as other men. Here, as in all its other judgments upon Christianity, the world is completely fooled by appearances, for it cannot see that these believing ones are "hid with Christ in God."

The man of true faith may live in the absolute assurance that his steps are ordered by the Lord. For him, misfortune is outside the bounds of possibility. He cannot be torn from this earth one hour ahead of the time which God has appointed, and he cannot be detained on earth one moment after God is done with him here. He is not a waif of the wide world, a foundling of time and space, but a saint of the Lord and the darling of His particular care.

All this is not mere dreaming, not a comforting creed woven as a garment to warm the shivering hearts of lonely, frightened souls in a dark and unfriendly world. Rather it is of the essence of truth, a fair summation of the teaching of the Bible on the subject and should be received reverently and joyously along with everything else which is taught in the Scriptures of truth.

> Here then I doubt no more,
> But in His pleasure rest,
> Whose wisdom, love and truth, and power
> Engage to make me blest.

Credulity versus Faith

C REDULITY AND FAITH are like toadstools and mushrooms respectively, near enough in appearance to be mistaken for each other, but so wholly unlike that their effects are exactly opposite.

The true man of faith is seldom credulous, and the credulous man seldom has real faith. Faith belongs to the simple-hearted, credulity to the simple-minded. They are worlds apart. The one honors God by believing His promises against all evidence; the other is a child of superstition and honors nobody. Rather, he reveals untidy mental habits and lack of spiritual insight.

It is astonishing what some people will believe when they get going. They properly hold it a sin to doubt the Bible, so they refuse to doubt anything that is served up along with the Bible, however ridiculous and unscriptural it may be. If the story has a flavor of wonder about it, these uncritical friends will accept it without question and repeat it in an awed voice with much solemn shaking of the bowed head. Multiply such people in any given church, and you have a perfect soil for the growth of every kind of false teaching and fanatical excess.

We need to cultivate a healthy skepticism toward everything that cannot be supported by the plain teaching of the Bible. Belief is faith only when it has God's revealed truth for its object; beyond that it may be fully as injurious as unbelief itself.

Many of the stories brought forward to justify the ways of God to men actually prove nothing except the unsoundness of the speaker's intellectual fiber. Yet if all chimney-corner Scripture and old wives' tales were forbidden, many a preacher would have to get out of the ministry. It is a deep pity that the Christian public must be forced to listen to so much nonsense and be helpless to do anything about it.

The point is, the Word of God needs no support from men. It stands alone, strong and majestic as the Matterhorn. When we call in the aid of childish stories and shaky illustrations to prove its truth, we do no more than to reveal our hidden unbelief and air our weak credulity.

The Bible:
the Book of Life

THE BIBLE IS UNIQUE AMONG BOOKS, which means simply that no book has been produced just like it.

The Bible is not a book of history, though it contains much history, and all it does contain is authentic. It is not a book of science, though all its pronouncements upon the facts usually falling into the category of science are accurate and trustworthy. It is not a book of biography, though its biographical sketches are easily the most inspiring in the world. It is not a book of philosophy, though it is the sum of all that is deep and sound philosophy. It is not a book of astronomy, though its references to the sun and the stars rate among the loftiest sayings ever recorded. It is not a book of psychology, though its knowledge of the workings of the human mind astonishes the reader and lays bare his soul. It is not strictly a book of theology, though it is the source of all the true theology this fallen world will ever know.

What, then, is the Bible? It is the Book of Life. "The words that I speak unto you," said our Lord, "they are spirit, and they are life."

The Bible is a life-bringing and a life-giving book. It is not primarily concerned with any department of human thought for its own sake. If the Bible speaks about the rainbow, it is that we may be reminded of God's covenant of mercy with mankind. If it tells the story of Abraham, it does so that we may learn to know the place of faith in our relation to God. If it points us to the moon and the stars, it is that we may know now frail we are. If it talks about the birds, it is to teach us to trust our Heavenly Father without fear or doubting. It tells us about hell not to satisfy our morbid curiosity, but that we may steer our feet far from its terrors. It tells us about heaven that we may be prepared to enter there. It writes the history of human disgrace that we may learn the value of divine grace. It warns in order that it may turn our feet away from the paths that go down to the path of destruction. It rebukes in order that we may see our own faults and be delivered from them.

Volumes could be written in praise of the Holy Bible without using one word too many. President Woodrow Wilson once said that the Bible is a book of such importance that no one unacquainted with it can be said to be an educated man, and one who is familiar with it can be said to be uneducated. Sir Walter Scott, when he was dying, called for "the book." A servant inquired which of his thousands of volumes he meant, and the great man replied, "The Bible, of course. For a dying man there can be no other book." Even the skeptic, George Bernard Shaw, during the last years of his life, kept a Bible near him and never traveled without carrying a copy along with him.

We should all have several Bibles: a well-bound reference Bible for study and a large-print, plain-text Bible for devotional reading. That many at least. And if we can afford it (and we can if we will cut down somewhere else), we should have a good modern translation or two. There are dozens of them. Their chief value is to stimulate interest by affording a change of style and to throw sidelights upon the test of the familiar King James Version.

Money invested in Bibles is money well spent. Time spent in reading the Bible is not likely to be time wasted. The Bible is the supreme gift for friends and loved ones. Words spoken in favor of the Bible are good words and, if they should fall upon the right ears, might prove to be "apples of gold in pictures of silver."

4

Autumn Winds

A UTUMN WINDS are blowing again.
The fall of the year brings with it a world of emotions as rich and varied as the notes of an organ. The spring is more stimulating and fuller of expectation, but there is about the fall a quiet strength which the spring lacks. It is not a wonder that so many serious-minded people love the fall,

> When the sound of dropping nuts is heard, though
> the trees are still,
> And twinkle in the smoky light the waters of
> the rill.

To the farmer, the first signs of autumn bring a warm sense of well-being. He no longer wonders whether his crops will turn out well. The full shocks of corn, the yellow pumpkins smiling between them, the high-piled haymows and the full silos assure him that God's summer has been good to him, and his work has been rewarded.

It is about this time of year, too, that a goodly number of men become strangely affected and begin to look off across the fields with an eager light in their eyes. For hunting season will soon be in, and the sound of gunfire and the baying of dogs will make sweet music over the hills and across the meadows. Not everyone hears this call out of the blue mists and the briar patches, but those who do need no one to interpret. They respond like the wild duck to the migratory instinct. After the first few days of absent-mindedness, they may be seen searching about for their old hunting coat or carefully polishing up their favorite gun, while the smell of fine oil mingles with the fragrance of burning leaves everywhere.

That is the fall for some people. And who would say that it is not good? Maybe it is one of the few innnocent things left in the world now.

The women are not likely to be affected these falls days the same as the men, but neither can they wholly escape the spell of autumn. In the country, the landscape is afire with color as the oak and the maple put on their last display of beauty before they go to sleep for the long winter. And those women who live pent-up in great cities may still enjoy something of the wonder of nature, if in nothing else than the sight of asters in the park or in a touch of goldenrod along the path in some chance vacant lot between the buildings.

We are not much given to moralizing on natural objects, but who can fail to notice the parallel between God's great lovely world and the little tribes of flesh and blood who inhabit it? Is it not plain that every human being runs through the same stages as the seasons? Spring, the time of childhood and youth when all the world is big with promise, a promise which the later years invariably fail to keep. Summer, the period of full power when life multiplies and it is hard to believe that it can ever end. Autumn, with its repose after toil, a gracious tapering off of our fuller powers, a kindly preparation for our longer rest. Winter, when the leaves have dropped away and the last sign of life has disappeared. Then only faith remains to assure us that there will be for us a bright tomorrow.

To the man out of Christ, the fall of the year, in spite of its many charms, must surely bring with it a deep and hidden terror. For it speaks of the approaching end, the time when it may be said, "The summer is ended, and we are not saved." It would be good indeed if the autumn winds could preach to the lost soul of the brevity of life and the long winter ahead.

The true Christian will not be saddened by the winds that herald the approach of winter. Like the wise ant he has made his preparation, and while the gusty tempest howls over him, he will sleep sweet in Christ while the circle of the heavens moves on toward the consummation of all things of which Moses and the prophets have spoken.

Happy man who knows that everything is well with him and that he will be among the blessed in that day when the breath of Jesus, like a breeze of spring, shall stir the sleeping dead to life again after the long night.

CHAPTER

5

Humility Wins Where Force Cannot

IN THE KINGDOM OF HEAVEN, weak things become mighty and mighty things often prove to be useless. God seeth not as man seeth, and the things that are held in high esteem among men may be scorned by the Most High God, maker of heaven and earth.

That carnal courage so prized in the kingdom of Adam may be the direct cause of constant and humiliating defeat among Christians. God will not be under the necessity of using fleshly means to accomplish His spiritual ends. The bold "strength of character" which helps men to forge to the front, to get the best jobs, to overawe their opponents, may stand squarely in the way of all efforts to progress in the life of the Spirit. God still gives courage to the faint, and He knoweth the proud afar off.

From Adam we inherit the instinct to meet our enemies head on, to try to win by direct assault, and it is only after many shocking failures that we learn that victories are not so won in the realm of the spiritual. The carnal approach usually does little more than to alienate the enemy still further from us, and worse than all, it puts us in a position where God cannot help us. The enemy never quite knows how to deal with a humble man; he is so used to dealing with proud, stubborn people that a meek man upsets his timetable. And furthermore, the man of true humility has God fighting on his side—who can win against God?

Strange as it may seem, we often win over our enemies only after we have first been soundly defeated by the Lord Himself. God often conquers our enemies by conquering us. He defeated Esau by defeating Jacob the night before on the bank of the Jabbok. The conquest of Esau took place in his brother Jacob. It is often so. When God foresees that we must meet a deadly opponent, he assures our victory by bringing us down in humbleness at His own feet. After that, everything is easy. We have put ourselves in a position where God can fight for us, and in a situation like that, the outcome is decided from eternity.

A Word to the Men about the Women

IT MIGHT BE A HUMBLING experience for some of us men to be allowed to see just how much of lasting spiritual value is being done by the women of the churches. As in the days of His flesh, Christ still has devout women who follow Him gladly and minister unto Him. The masculine tendency to discount these "elect ladies" does not speak too well for the male members of the spiritual community. A little humility might better become us, and a bit of plain gratitude as well.

If prayer is (as we believe it is) an integral part of the total divine scheme of things and must be done if the will of God is to be done, then the prayers of the thousands of women who meet each week in our churches is of inestimable value to the kingdom of God. More power to them, and may their number increase tenfold.

Let us beware, as men, however, that we do not fall into the weak habit of depending upon the women of the church to do our praying for us. If our work prevents us, as it normally does, from having prayer meetings during the day, let us make up for it in some way and see to it that we pray as much as we should.

Prayer is not a work that can be allocated to one or another group in the church. It is everybody's responsibility; it is everybody's privilege. Prayer is the respiratory function of the church; without it we suffocate and die at last, like a living body deprived of the breath of life. Prayer knows no sex, for the soul has no sex, and it is the soul that must pray. Women can pray, and their prayers will be answered; but so can man, and so should men if they are to fill the place God has given them in the church.

Let us watch that we do not slide imperceptibly to a state where the women do the praying and the men run the churches. Men who do not pray have no right to direct church affairs. We believe in the leadership of men within the spiritual community of the saints, but that leadership should be won by spiritual worth.

Leadership requires vision, and whence will vision come except from hours spent in the presence of God in humble and fervent prayer? All things else being equal, a praying woman will know the will of God for the church far better than a prayerless man.

We do not here advocate the turning of the churches over to the women, but we do advocate a recognition of proper spiritual qualifications for leadership among the men if they are to continue to decide the direction the churches shall take. The accident of being a man is not enough. Spiritual manhood alone qualifies.

"Choose seven men from among you," commanded the apostles, "who are known to be full of the Spirit and wisdom. We will turn this responsibility over to them" (Acts 6:3). The men chosen as a consequence of this directive became the first deacons of the church. Thus the direction of certain church affairs was put into the hands of men spiritually qualified. Should we not maintain the same standards today?

There Are No Insignificant Christians

ONE OF THE HEAVIEST THOUGHTS that can visit the human heart is the insignificance of the average man. Seen against the long procession of the ages and the countless multitudes of people who have inhabited the earth, we are each one no more than a grain of sand on the wide seashore.

It takes some reflection to make this appear to our minds as it really is. The human ego may be counted upon to accent our individual worth and to give a false permanence to what is anything but permanent. A man in his pride may feel himself to be so important that it is hard for him to visualize the world as continuing to endure after he is removed from the scene; but all we need to do is to wait. Time will grind him to dust and toss him to the winds; his friends will disappear one by one from their old familiar haunts, and there will be no one left to remember him. The passing generations will sift over him layer upon layer of forgetfulness, and he will no longer have any earthly meaning. He will cease to be a name and will become merely a statistic.

This consideration, if no other, should dispose us

to embrace the message of Christ. That message is so full and so comprehensive that it is never possible to state in one paragraph or one page or one volume all that it is. It is doubtful, in fact, whether all the world could contain the books if the whole wonder of the gospel were to be written. But not the least among the benefits of the Cross is its dignification of the individual.

No matter how insignificant he may have been before, a man becomes significant the moment he has had an encounter with the Son of God. When the Lord lays His hand upon a man, that man ceases at once to be ordinary. He immediately becomes extraordinary, and his life takes on cosmic significance. The angels in heaven take notice of him and go forth to become his ministers (Hebrews 1:14). Though the man had before been only one of the faceless multitude, a mere cipher in the universe, an invisible dust grain blown across endless wastes—now he gets a face and a name and a place in the scheme of meaningful things. Christ knows His own sheep "by name."

A young preacher introduced himself to the pastor of a great metropolitan church with the words, "I am just the pastor of a small church upcountry." "Son," replied the wise minister, "there are no small churches." And there are no unknown Christians, no insignificant sons of God. Each one signifies, each is a "sign" drawing the attention of the Triune God day and night upon him. The faceless man has a face, the nameless man a name, when Jesus picks him out of the multitude and calls him to Himself.

No doubt we grieve our Lord by thinking of ourselves as less than we are in the plan of God. In ourselves we are nothing, and the vast gulf of forgetfulness toward which we were heading was the proper place for us. We had earned no share in God's interest, no place in His affection; our sins had forfeited any claim we might have had upon God as Creator. But the blood of the everlasting covenant has changed all that. Our claim now is that of a child upon his Father. We have a right in the Father's household, and we can sit down at His table without fear or embarrassment. In the kingdom of God we signify.

The Tragedy of Waste

To EACH OF US God has issued a certain store as it has pleased Him: to one more, to another less. And since God owes us nothing, anything He gives us may be put down to His unearned generosity. The man with a smaller store dare not complain against God for having given him less than his neighbor received. God's gifts are not debts which He pays us, but gratuities bestowed out of pure mercy.

One thing taught large in the Holy Scriptures is that while God gives His gifts freely. He will require a strict accounting of them at the end of the road. Each man is personally responsible for his store, be it large or small, and will be required to explain his use of it before the judgment seat of Christ.

The "store" is nothing new, just the old familiar list of human possessions: time, talents, earthly goods, opportunities. Though they are as common as the grass beside the path, the waste of them constitutes one of life's most appalling tragedies.

First, there is *time*. None of us has much of it. The crow that flaps across the meadow will probably live longer than the oldest one of us. The tree that shades the sleepy cow in the pasture may have looked down on our grandfather when he was a boy, and it may remain to watch the passing of our children's children. And that we have so small a store of time constitutes a powerful reason for our making the most of what we have. Yet how many hours have we spent doing nothing or doing the wrong thing. Our cynical waste of precious time could be a reason for our not having more of it given to us, who knows? Jesus once said, "Gather up the fragments that remain, that nothing be lost."

Time wasted is lost beyond recall. While we sympathize with the emotional content of the old song, "Backward, turn backward, O time, in your flight," it is yet hard to conceive of a more futile appeal. Time does not run backward. The old man does not become young, the young man becomes old. So it has always been and so it will ever be. The bird of time flies past us and is gone; "the leaves of life keep falling one by one, the wine of life keeps oozing drop by drop." We must work while it is called today.

Then there are *talents*. These are included in the total store granted us by our Heavenly Father. Whether we have one talent or many, we must render up account finally, and the factor that will decide for us is not how many talents we had but what we did with them. The story of the man who hid his talent in the ground makes disquieting reading for the careless Christian who is failing to make use of his gifts. Some with modest gifts have made a brilliant record of spiritual achievement; others with far greater abilities have played through the summer of life like the grasshopper in the fable and have let their gifts lie unused while time idled by. This, we repeat, is tragedy, and that it is common does not make it any the less tragic.

Money is another item. American Christians make so much of it and spend it so lavishly that they have unconsciously learned to take it as a matter for granted and have forgotten that they will be strictly judged for their use of it. The Lord still stands by the treasury and observes what is placed therein. This has been turned into a joke by humorists who are ready always to find something funny in every reference to money. But it is safe to predict that there will be little laughter when the Lord with eyes like a flame of fire looks into our accounts and makes His just audit. We might do well right now to do a little auditing ourselves while there is time to make amends for our failures.

God has also given us a wealth of *opportunities*. An opportunity may be defined as a providential circumstance which permits us to turn our time, our money and our talents to account. Of all gifts this is the most common, and it is the one which makes the other gifts of value to us and to mankind. The wise Christian will watch for opportunities to do good, to speak the life-bringing word to sinners, to pray the rescuing prayer of intercession.

The foe of opportunity is preoccupation. Just when God sends along a chance to turn a great victory for mankind, some of us are too busy puttering around to notice it. Or we notice it when it is too late. The old Greeks said that opportunity had a forelock but was close-shaven behind; if a man missed grabbing for her as she approached, he would reach for her in vain after she had passed.

Possibly the worst effect of waste is the mental

habit it creates. To allow time or money or talents to go to waste is to do something harmful to ourselves. It is to injure ourselves inside where it is most serious.

9

Success Is Costly

SUCCESS IN ANY FIELD is costly, but the man who will pay the price can have it.

The concert pianist must become a slave to his instrument; four hours, five hours each day he must sit at the keyboard. The scientist must live for his work. The philosopher must devote himself to thought, the scholar to his books. The price may seem excessively heavy, but there are some who consider the reward worthwhile.

The laws of success operate also in the higher field of the soul—spiritual greatness has its price. Eminence in the things of the Spirit demands a devotion to these things more complete than most of us are willing to give. But the law cannot be escaped. If we would be holy we know the way; the law of holy living is before us. The prophets of the Old Testament, the apostles of the New and, more than all, the sublime teachings of Christ are there to tell us how to succeed.

Through a misunderstanding of the doctrine of grace, some shy away from the idea that the laws of God operate in the kingdom of heaven. They make a radical cleavage of things natural from things spiritual and refuse to allow any relation between them. To do this, they must overlook the fact that

the Bible writers in all their teachings drew copi-
ously from the wells of common life. For them, all
nature spoke God's message—from the homely
blade of grass beside the path to the sun and the
stars in the heavens above. Kings and farmers of-
fered light on the ways of God; the ant and the
sparrow had their contribution to make; the dul-
lard was there as a horrible example, and the slug-
gard sitting in his ruined house or walking between
the rows of his scrubby corn served as a melan-
choly example of what laziness could do to the man
who would not conquer it. The householder who
began to build without having figured the cost, the
king who started war without knowing that he
could win it, the farmer who put his hand to the
plow and then changed his mind and looked
back—all these are in the Bible, and they all say the
same thing: that spirituality has a solid core of in-
telligence in it, that success in the life of faith requires common sense, hard work and wise cooper-
ation with the law of cause and effect.

The amount of loafing practiced by the average
Christian in spiritual things would ruin a concert
pianist if he allowed himself to do the same thing in
the field of music. The idle puttering around that
we see in church circles would end the career of a
big league pitcher in one week. No scientist could
solve his exacting problem if he took as little interest in it as the rank and file of Christians take in the
art of being holy. The nation whose soldiers were
as soft and undisciplined as the soldiers of the
churches would be conquered by the first enemy
that attacked it. Triumphs are not won by men in
easy chairs. Success is costly.

If we would progress spiritually, we must separate ourselves unto the things of God and concentrate upon them to the exclusion of a thousand things the worldly man considers important. We must cultivate God in the solitudes and the silence; we must make the kingdom of God the sphere of our activity and labor in it like a farmer in his field, like a miner in the earth.

Dismissing Distractions

FAILING IN HIS FRONTAL ATTACKS upon the child of God, Satan often turns to more subtle means of achieving his evil purpose. He resorts to devious methods in his attempt to divert the Christian from carrying out the task God has committed to him. He often succeeds by involving the saint in some other lesser occupation and so distracting him.

Nehemiah, the good, rose up from his weeping to do something about a vision God had laid on his heart. Under divine providence, he was soon transported from Shushan to his beloved city, Jerusalem, armed with authority and equipped with materials to rebuild the ruined city.

When Nehemiah's purpose and plans were made known to the men of Jerusalem, they raised the determined shout, "Let us rise up and build."

The first device of the "enemy," upon hearing of the undertaking, was to heap ridicule on the whole plan. Sanballat, Tobiah and Geshem laughed Nehemiah and his helpers to scorn. Undeterred, Nehemiah replied with firm assurance, "The God of heaven, he will prosper us." And the work went on according to plan.

After all other means had failed to hinder the reconstruction, the conspirators tried to arrange for a conference with Nehemiah. The man of God saw in this an evil purpose to do him mischief and divert him from his monumental work. His reply to the would-be mischief-makers is classic, and might well be adopted for the all-time stock reply to all such overtures: "I am carrying on a great project and cannot go down. Why should the work stop while I leave it and go down to you?" (Nehemiah 6:3).

The great task to which God had called Nehemiah was so important that every other consideration must be waived. Would that we might have such an overpowering sense of being about our Father's business and be so impressed with the grandeur of our task that we would reject every suggestion of the evil one that would bid us take up some lesser pursuit. Let us rout him with the words that date back to 445 B.C., and which cannot be improved upon: "I am carrying on a great project and cannot go down."

Satan's distracting words often come from the most unexpected quarters. Martha would call Mary away from sitting at the feet of the Master. Sometimes, if we are not careful, our best friend may distract us. Or it might be some very legitimate activity. This day's bustle and hurly-burly would too often and too soon call us away from Jesus' feet. These distractions must be immediately dismissed, or we shall know only the "barrenness of busyness."

The multiplying agencies and the extraneous activities of much of the current gospel "programing" may distract us if we are not wary and lead us into some meandering bypath that comes to a dead end. Our genius is preserved by sticking at the task of worldwide evangelization that God has called us to by the tried and proven methods that God has blessed, thereby avoiding the slough of an effete denominationalism on the one hand and unproductive, fevered activity on the other.

In a world like ours, we need to master the art and keep at the business of dismissing distractions.

A Christian Cannot Afford to Blame

A LIFETIME OF OBSERVATION, Bible reading and prayer has led to the conclusion that the only thing that can hinder a Christian's progress is the Christian himself.

The true child of God can live and grow in circumstances that are wholly unfavorable to such life and growth. Outward circumstances can help little or none in a Christian's spiritual life. The whole philosophy of the spiritual way requires us to believe this.

For this reason, it is always bad to blame anyone or anything for our spiritual or moral failures. God has so ordered things that His children may grow as successfully in the middle of a desert as in the most fruitful land. It is necessary that this should be so, seeing that the very world itself is a field where nothing good can grow except by some kind of miracle. The old hymn asks the rhetorical question, "Is this vile world a friend to grace, to help me on to God?" And the implied answer is no. Grace operates without the help of the world.

It matters little how twisted a man's life may be, there is hope for him if he will but establish a right attitude toward God and refuse to admit any other element into his spiritual thinking. *God and I;* here is the beginning and the end of personal religion. Faith refuses to acknowledge that there is or ever can be a third party to this holy relation.

Attitude is all-important. Let the soul take a quiet attitude of faith and love toward God, and from there on the responsibility is God's. He will make good on His commitments. There is not on earth a lonely spot where a Christian cannot live and be spiritually victorious if God sends him there. He carries his own climate with him or has it supplied supernaturally when he arrives. Since he is not dependent for his spiritual health upon local moral standards or current religious beliefs, he lives through a thousand earthly changes, unaffected by any of them. He has a private supply from above and is in reality a little world within a world and very much of a wonder to the rest of creation.

Because this is true, we can easily see why we should never blame our spiritual failures on others. The habit of seeking weak consolation by blaming our poor showing on unfavorable circumstances is a damaging evil and should not for one moment be tolerated. To live a lifetime believing that our inner weakness was the result of an external situation and then find at the last that we ourselves were to blame—that is too painful to be contemplated.

Ten thousand enemies cannot stop a Christian, cannot even slow him down, if he meets them in a attitude of complete trust in God. They will become to him like the atmosphere that resists the airplane, but which because the plane's designer knew how to take advantage of that resistance, actually lifts the plane aloft and holds it there for a journey of 2,000 miles. What would have been an enemy to the plane becomes a helpful servant to aid it on its way.

The main thing is this: we should never blame anyone or anything for our defeats. No matter how evil their intentions may be, they are altogether unable to harm us until we begin to blame them and use them as excuses for our own unbelief. Then they become potent to do us injury; nevertheless, we are to blame and not they.

If this should seem like a bit of theorizing, remember that always the greatest Christians have come out of hard times and tough situations. Tribulations actually worked for their spiritual perfection in that they taught them to trust not in themselves but in the Lord who raised the dead. They learned that the enemy could not block their progress unless they surrendered to the urgings of the flesh and began to complain. And slowly, they learned to stop complaining and start praising. It is that simple—and it works!

Truth Brings
Problems, Too

THE TRUTH RESOLVES SOME difficulties and creates others.

"The truth shall make you free"; that is, free from the woes, the yokes, the burdens which sin imposes.

Yet that same truth brings problems of another kind. It cannot be otherwise, since we are forced to entertain truth in a world dedicated to the lie. Human society is in a quiet conspiracy against the truth as far as it touches spiritual and moral things. The soul dedicated to God's truth is never popular with the multitudes. They make him pay for his love of truth. And that creates a problem for him.

Wherever and whenever truth gets itself incarnated in a man, that man is sure to become the target for every kind of opposition from the casual barbed insult of a professed friend to the carefully prepared campaign of the avowed enemy. The problem this creates for the man of truth is how to accept these attacks in the spirit of charity, how to keep cool and patient when all his old natural reflexes urge him to strike back with every weapon at his command.

The man whom Christ illuminates with His message has eyes, and that resolves the old difficulty of blindness; but he must use his new eyes in a blind world, and that creates another problem. The world in its blindness resents his claim to sight and will go to any lengths to discredit the claim. The truth of Christ brings assurance and so removes the former problem of fear and uncertainty, but that assurance will be interpreted as bigotry by the fear-ridden multitudes. And sooner or later this misunderstanding will get the man of God into trouble. And so with many other of the blessed benefits of the gospel. As long as we remain in this twisted world, these benefits will create their own problems. We cannot escape them.

But no instructed Christian will complain. He will rather accept his problems as opportunities for the exercise of spiritual virtues. He will turn them into useful disciplines for the purification of his life and will rejoice that he is permitted to suffer with his Lord. For however severe may be a Christian's trials, they cannot last very long, and the blessed fruit they bear will last while the ages endure.

Why Some Christians Are Disliked

SOMETIMES WE CHRISTIANS are opposed and per-secuted for reasons other than our godliness. We like to think it is our spirituality that irritates people, when in reality, it may be our personality.

True, the spirit of this world is opposed to the Spirit of God; he that is born after the flesh will persecute him that is born of the Spirit. But making all allowances, it is still true that some Christians get into trouble through their faults instead of through their likeness to the character of Christ. We may as well admit this and do something about it. No good can come from trying to hide our un-pleasant and annoying dispositional traits behind a verse of Scripture.

It is one of the strange facts of life that gross sins are often less offensive and always more attractive than spiritual ones. The world can tolerate a drunk-ard or a glutton or a smiling braggart but will turn in savage fury against the man of outwardly right-eous life who is guilty of those refined sins, which he does not recognize as sins, but which may be more exceeding sinful than the sins of the flesh.

Any act gains in power as it moves inward toward

the heart. For this reason, the sins of the spirit are more iniquitous than those of the body. This was illustrated boldly by the attitude of our Lord toward these two kinds of sins and the corresponding two classes of sinners. He was the friend of publicans and harlots and the enemy of the Pharisees.

All sin is sinful and will be fatal to the soul if it is not forgiven and cleansed away. But for intensity of iniquity, the sins of the spirit are in a class by themselves. Yet they are the very sins which are most likely to be committed by religious people.

The careless sinner expresses himself overtly and so "releases" the moral tension; the religious sinner is not likely so to do. He scorns outward acts of wickedness and drives his sin inward to the sanctuary of his soul where it remains in a state of high compression. The notorious unloveliness of many religious people can be explained in this way.

It might be a shock to some of us if we could know why we are disliked and why our testimony is rejected so violently. Could it be that we are guilty of a deep sinfulness of disposition that we just cannot keep hidden? Arrogance, lack of charity, contempt, self-righteousness, religious snobbery, fault-finding—and all this kept under careful restraint and disguised by a pious smile and synthetic good humor. This sort of thing is *felt* rather than understood by those who touch us in everyday life. They do not know why they cannot stand us, but *we* are sure that the reason is our exalted state of spirituality! Perilous comfort. Deep heart searching and prolonged repentance would be better.

Yet let us not assume that if we are persecuted it

is because of our faults. The opposite may be the fact. They may hate us because they first hated Christ, and if that is so, then blessed are we indeed. The point is, let us take nothing for granted. We may be better than we think we are, but the likelihood is not overwhelming. Humility is best.

If Christ Carries
the Burden

IF A BURDEN IS LAID on my back and another immediately takes it off and carries it himself," said
Meister Eckhart, "it can make no difference to me
whether it is one or a hundred pounds."

In the Scriptures, there would seem to be three
kinds of burdens recognized. First, the burden of
loving help which we are admonished to give to
others: "Carry each other's burdens, and in this
way you will fulfill the law of Christ" (Galatians
6:2). Secondly, the burden of moral responsibility
which no one can shift to another: "For each one
should carry his own load" (Galatians 6:5). Thirdly,
the burden resulting from our fallen state, consist-
ing of sin, fear, worry, disappointments, sorrows,
remorse, bitter memories and self-accusations.

The first burden never harmed a soul. The second may even be a source of quiet comfort if our
hearts are right. It is the third sort that ages and
shrivels and kills. And there is no valid reason for
our carrying it (or them, for there are many of this
kind). "Cast your cares on the Lord and he will
sustain you" (Psalm 55:22). That was what the
good Eckhart had in mind when he suggested that

no burden would be heavier than any other if the Lord carried it for us.

Unnecessary burdens are crushing the life out of people every day. Mental institutions are overflowing and psychiatrists are doing a rushing business because the burden of living is getting to be more than we can bear. Civilization has not made our lot easier except in things pertaining to the body; the burdens of the heart are growing more numerous, and science has found no remedy. The silky voice of the practitioner may soothe the mind for a time, but the disease is too deep to yield itself to such inadequate measures.

Surely we could live longer and better and be far happier and more useful if we could learn to cast our burdens upon the Lord. Then it would not matter how heavy they were, for He would carry them for us.

"Love Is the Will To, the Intention"

Among the innocent victims of this effete and degenerate age, there is none so pure and so beautiful as *love*.

Next to the word *God* with its various forms, there is no word so fair in all the language. Yet it may be said without qualification that this beautiful word has so suffered in the house of its friends as now to be scarcely recognizable. For the great mass of mankind, love has lost its divine meaning. The novelist, the playwright, the psychoanalyst, the writer of popular love songs, have abused this fair being too long. For filthy lucre, they have dragged her through the sewers of the human mind until she appears to the world as no more than a blowzy and bloated strumpet for whom no one any longer has the least trace of respect, the mention of whose name brings no more than a wink or an embarrassed simper. By losing the divine content from the concept of love, modern man now has remaining only what we might expect—a brazen-faced dowd whom he courts at all hours of the day and night with songs that should make a chimpanzee blush.

Civilized man has brought about this tragic fall by associating love with sex exclusively and then popularizing the error by every means at his command. Millions of young people today are wholly unable to think of love except in terms of the disgraceful promiscuity of Hollywood. Newspapers now report the numerous marriages of the movie crowd by number: "It was the third marriage for her; his fourth." And if it were not so tragic for everyone concerned, it would be hugely comical to read of a movie star being interviewed by the press and solemnly assuring the public that she is not at the moment "in love." Such a use of the word is completely degraded and smacks more of the beasts than of men made in the image of God.

For the millions, love is an emotional attraction, nothing more, as unstable and as unpredictable as sheet lightning. The Bible teaches, on the contrary, that true love is a benevolent principle and *is under the control of the will.* If love were merely an emotion, how could God command us to love Him, or to love our neighbor? No one can "fall in love" at the command of another, if falling in love means getting seized suddenly with a fit of love as one might be hit with a charge of electricity or caught with a severe spasm of coughing.

"Love," said Meister Eckhart, "is the will to, the intention." By that definition, it is possible to obey the divine command to love our neighbor. We may not in a thousand years be able to feel a surge of emotion toward certain "neighbors," but we can go before God and solemnly will to love them, and the love will come. By prayer and an application of the inworking power of God, we may set our faces to will the good of our neighbor and not his evil all the days of our lives, and that is love. The emotion may follow, or there may be no appreciable change in our feelings toward him, but the intention is what matters. We will his peace and prosperity and put ourselves at his disposal to help him in every way possible, even to the laying down of our lives for his sake.

Love, then, is a principle of good will and is to a large extent under our control. That it can be fanned into a blazing fire is not denied here. Certainly God's love for us has a mighty charge of feeling in it, but beneath it all is a set principle that wills our peace. Probably the love of God for mankind was never more beautifully stated than by the angel at the birth of Christ: "Glory to God in the highest, and on earth peace to man on whom his favor rests."

God's Side versus the Wrong Side

WHENEVER AND WHEREVER there is a controversy between God and a man, God is always right and the man always wrong. "So that you may be proved right in your words and prevail in your judging" (Psalm 51:4).

The only way any man can be right is to come over onto God's side. Whoever sticks to his own side is forever wrong.

The points at which God's way and man's intersect are likely to be four (though there may be others), and we will usually find our differences with God to occur somewhere in these four areas.

First, *our thoughts.* Divine inspiration has declared that the thoughts of man are vain, and in the prophecy of Isaiah, God sets His case before us so plainly that comment is hardly necessary: "For my thoughts are not your thoughts, neither are your ways my ways," declares the Lord. "As the heavens are higher than the earth, so are my ways higher than your ways and my thoughts than your thoughts" (Isaiah 55:8–9).

Second, our *moral standards.* There are probably as many ideas of righteousness as there are people in the world, and it would be futile to argue that one is better than another. The test is not which code is best but whether or not any code agrees with the Scriptures. In the Christian Scriptures, the Lord of the whole earth declares His own moral will for mankind, and it is profound wisdom to seek it and conform to it. Otherwise, we are at the mercy of our own deceitful hearts. For all men of faith, God's will is righteousness. The believing soul will not argue about it; he will accept it and bring the controversy to an end.

The third point of possible controversy is in our *way of life*. This embraces the whole of our lives on earth as decided by our basic moral ideas. Our way of life is simply our moral code in its daily outflow.

The fourth is *our plans*. The Christian who has in principle accepted God's truth as his standard of conduct and has submitted himself to Christ as his Lord, may yet be tempted to lay his own plans and even fight for them when they are challenged by the Word of God or the inner voice of the Spirit. We humans are a calculating, planning race, and we like to say, "Tomorrow I will . . ." But our Heavenly Father knows us too well to trust our way to our own planning, so He very often submits His own plans to us and requires that we accept them. Right there a controversy is sometimes stirred up between the soul and God. But we had better not insist on our own way. It will always be bad for us in the long run. God's way is best.

Among men, questions usually have more than one side; sometimes they have many. Pros and cons are often balanced so finely against each other that it is virtually impossible to know where the right lies. But with God there is only one side. God's side is good and holy and all other sides are wrong, the degree and seriousness of the wrong increasing as we move away from the center of God's will.

Our desire for moral self-preservation should dictate that we come over immediately onto God's side and stay there even if (as is likely) it may result in our being out of accord with man's philosophies and man's moral codes. We cannot win when we work against God, and we cannot lose when we work with Him.

Now, how can we know for certain which side is God's side? No one in this late day should need to ask that question, but since it is being asked in all sincerity by many, we are glad to give the answer. There is a Book which says of itself, "And God spoke all these words," and about which it is said, "Beyond all question, the mystery of godliness is great: He appeared in a body, was vindicated by the Spirit, was seen by angels, was preached among the nations, was believed on in the world, was taken up to glory" (1 Timothy 3:16). Acquaintance with this Book will bring light to all dark paths and show us the right side of all questions. Of course, that Book is the Bible.

What glory gilds the sacred page,
  Majestic like the sun!
It gives a light to every age;
  It gives, but borrows none.

Praying without Condition

JULIANA OF NORWICH at the beginning of her wonderful Christian life addressed a prayer to her Savior and then added the wise words, "And this I ask without any condition."

It was that last sentence that gave power to the rest of her prayer and brought the answer in mighty poured-out floods as the years went by. God could answer her prayer because He did not need to mince matters with her. She did not hedge her prayers around with disclaimers and provisos. She wanted certain things from God at any cost. God, as it were, had only to send her the bill. She would pay any price to get what she conceived to be good for her soul and glorifying to her Heavenly Father. That is real praying.

Many of us spoil our prayers by being too "dainty" with the Lord (as some old writer called it). We ask with the tacit understanding that the cost must be reasonable. After all, there is a limit to everything, and we do not want to be fanatical! We want the answer to be something added, not something taken away. We want nothing radical or out of the ordinary, and we want God to accommodate us at our convenience. Thus we attach a rider to every prayer, making it impossible for God to answer it.

In a world like ours, courage is an indispensable virtue. The coward may snivel in his corner, but the brave man takes the prize. And in the kingdom of God, courage is as necessary as it is in the world. The timid soul is as pitiable on his knees as he is in society.

When entering the prayer chamber, we must come filled with faith and armed with courage. Nowhere else in the whole field of religious thought and activity is courage so necessary as in prayer. The successful prayer must be one without condition. We must believe that God is love and that, being love, He cannot harm us but must ever do us good. Then we must throw ourselves before Him and pray with boldness for whatever we know our good and His glory require, and the cost is no object! Whatever He in His love and wisdom would assess against us, we will accept with delight because it pleased Him. Prayers like that cannot go unanswered. The character and reputation of God guarantee their fulfillment.

We should always keep in mind the infinite loving kindness of God. No one need fear to put his life in His hands. His yoke is easy; His burden is light.

O Lord, Turn Us Again to Thee!

IT IS MORE THAN PROBABLE that in the whole history of the United States there was never at any one time so much religious activity as there is today. And it is also very likely that there was never less true spirituality.

For some reason, religious activity and godliness do not always go together. To discover this, it is only necessary to observe the current religious scene. There is no lack of soul-winning effort surely, but many of the soul-winners give one the impression that they are little more than salesmen for a brand of Christianity that simply does not lead to saintliness.

If this should strike you as being uncharitable, make this little test: kneel down and read reverently the Sermon on the Mount. Let it get hold of your heart. Catch the spiritual "feeling" of it. Try to conceive what kind of person he or she would be who would embody its teachings. Then compare your conception with the product of the modern religious mill. You will find a wide world of difference both in conduct and in spirit. If the Sermon on the Mount is a fair description of the sort of person a Christian ought to be, then what are we to conclude about the multitudes who have "accepted" Christ but nevertheless exhibit not one moral or spiritual trait such as those described by our Lord?

Now, experience has prepared us for the rebuttal we will surely hear from tender-minded friends: "Who are we to judge? We must leave these professed Christians with the Lord and look to our own doorstep. And furthermore, we should be glad for any little bit of good that is being done and not spoil it by faultfinding."

All that sounds good, but it is an expression of a religious *laissez faire* which would stand carelessly by and permit the whole church of Christ to degenerate morally and spiritually without daring to raise a hand to help or a voice to warn. So did not the prophets. So did not Christ, or His apostles, or the Reformers; and so will not any man do who has seen heaven opened and beheld visions of God. Elijah could have kept his mouth shut and saved himself a lot of trouble. John the Baptist could have kept silent and saved his head; and every martyr might have pleaded *laissez faire* and died comfortably in his bed at a ripe old age. But in doing so, they would all have disobeyed God and laid themselves open to a severe judgment in the day of Christ.

The absence of spiritual devotion today is an omen and a portent. The modern church is all but contemptuous of the sober virtues—meekness, modesty, humility, quietness, obedience, self-effacement, patience. To be accepted now, religion must be in the popular mood. Consequently, much religious activity reeks with pride, display, self-assertion, self-promotion, love of gain and devotion to trivial pleasures.

It behooves us to take all this seriously. Time is running out for all of us. What is done must be done quickly. We have no right to lie idly by and let things take their course. A farmer who neglects his farm will soon lose it; a shepherd who fails to look after his flock will find the wolves looking after it for him. A misbegotten charity that allows the wolves to destroy the flock is not charity at all but indifference, rather, and should be known for what it is and dealt with accordingly.

It is time for Bible-believing Christians to begin to cultivate the sober graces and to live among men like sons of God and heirs of the ages. And this will take more than a bit of doing, for the whole world and a large part of the church is set to prevent it. But if God be for us, who can be against us?

Heresy among the Saints

HERESY IS NOT SO MUCH rejecting as selecting.
The heretic simply selects the parts of the
Scripture he wants to emphasize and lets the rest
go.

This is shown by the etymology of the word *heresy* and by the practice of the heretic. "Beware," an
editorial scribe of the 14th century warned his readers in the preface to a book. "Beware thou take not
one thing after thy affection and liking, and leave
another: for that is the condition of an heretique.
But take everything with other." The old scribe
knew well how prone we are to take to ourselves
those parts of the truth that please us and ignore
the other parts. And that is heresy.

Almost every cult with which we have any acquaintance practices this art of selecting and ignoring. The no-hell cults, for example, habitually
stress everything in the Bible that seems to support
their position and play down or explain away all
the passages that deal with eternal punishment.

But we do well to look closer to home. Proneness
to heresy is not confined to the cults. By nature, we
are all heretics. We who count ourselves to be in the
historic tradition of sound doctrine may in actual
practice become heretics after a sort. We may un-

consciously select for special attention such Scriptures as comfort and encourage us and pass over the ones that rebuke and warn us. This trap is so easy to fall into that we may be in it before we are aware.

Take, for instance, the "well-marked" Bible. It might be an illuminating experience to peep into one sometimes and note how the owner has underscored almost exclusively the passages that console him or that support his views on doctrine. We habitually love the verses that are easy on us and shy away from the ones that disturb us.

Undoubtedly God goes along with us as far as He can in this weak and one-sided treatment of the Holy Scriptures, but He cannot be pleased with this way of doing. Our Heavenly Father takes pleasure in seeing us develop and grow up spiritually. He does not want us to live entirely on a diet of sweet stuff. He gives us for our encouragement Isaiah 41, but He gives us also Matthew 23 and the book of Jude, and He expects us to read it all. The 8th chapter of Romans is one of the most elevating passages in the entire Bible, and its popularity is well deserved; but we need Second Peter as well, and we should not neglect to read it. When reading Paul's epistles, we should not stop with the doctrinal sections but should go on to read and ponder the bracing exhortations that follow. We should not stop with Romans 11; the rest of the epistle is also important, and if we would treat our souls fairly, we must give it the same attention we gave to the first 10 chapters.

Briefly, the health of our souls requires that we take the whole Bible as it stands and let it do its work in us. We cannot afford to be selective with anything so important as the Word of God and our own eternal future.

CHAPTER

20

On Bearing Others' Infirmities

OUR LOFTY IDEALISM WOULD argue that all Christians should be perfect, but a blunt realism forces us to admit that perfection is rare even among the saints. The part of wisdom is to accept our Christian brothers and sisters for what they are rather than for what they should be.

We do not wish to excuse the laziness of the saints or to provide carnality with a place to hide, but it is necessary that we face facts. And the plain fact is that the average Christian—even true Christian—is yet a long way from being like Christ in character and life. There is much that is imperfect about us, and it is fitting that we recognize it and call upon God for charity to put up with one another. The perfect church is not on this earth. The most spiritual church is sure to have in it some who are still bothered by the flesh.

An old Italian proverb says, "He that will have none but a perfect brother must resign himself to remain brotherless." However earnestly we may desire that our Christian brother go on toward perfection, we must accept him as he is and learn to get along with him. To treat an imperfect brother impatiently is to advertise our own imperfections.

55

The Apostle Paul wrote, "We who are strong ought to bear with the failings of the weak and not to please ourselves" (Romans 15:1). He thus plainly accepts the fact that there will be infirm people among the believing members of the spiritual community we call the local church. He tells us to bear them, or bear with them in their weakness.

Now who are the infirm persons in the church? How can we identify them? Not how can we find them, for they are sure to be easiest of all people to find. Their very infirmities make them conspicuous. The infirm brother is the one who has painful conscientious scruples about foods (Romans 14:1–2); or he has deep convictions about certain holy days (Romans 14:5–6); or his grasp of gospel truth is weak, and he is forced to support himself by various crutches which he may have found in some religious attic. To him these scruples are sacred; consequently, he is likely to try to force them upon everyone else, and in doing so he is pretty sure to make very much of a nuisance of himself. That is where the "strong" Christian gets opportunity to give his patience a workout. He dare not dismiss the overheated brother; he must bear with him in love, knowing that he too is of the company of the redeemed.

This brief list does not at all exhaust the number of infirmities we are likely to find in the Christian assembly. Who has not had to bear lovingly with a brother (or sister) who is afflicted with logorrhea, the incurable propensity to talk without pause or punctuation? That the talk is "religious" does not make it the less painful. And the unstable brother who spends his time either falling or getting up again, who is either leaping for joy or lying face down bewailing his hard lot—what church is there that does not have one or two such believers in it? Then there is the Mark Twain of the holy place, whose testimonies must always have their element of alleged humor; and to offset him somewhat is the man of heavy countenance who cannot smile and to whom a pleasantry is a mortal sin. Add to this list the sister whose prayers are accusations against the church or self-pitying complaints about the way she is being treated by other members of the flock.

What shall we do about these infirm brothers and sisters? If we deal with them according to their deserts, we may crush them beyond recovery. The thing to do is to accept them as crosses and bear them for Jesus' sake. In the great day when we have become like our Lord and have left all imperfections behind, we will not be sorry we endured patiently the infirmities of the weak.

21

Holy Men and
Holy Deeds

EMERSON COMPLAINS IN one his essays that society tends to overlook our essential humanity
and to think of us as *being* what we *do*. There
should be no farmers, he argues, or carpenters, or
painters; there should only be *men* who farm and
paint and do carpenter work.

This distinction is fine but vastly important, for
the most vital thing about any man is not what he
does or what he has but what he *is*. And first of all,
a man must be a man—that is, a human being free
in the earth, free to do anything his basic humanity
requires him to do. And apart from sin (which is a
moral abnormality, a disease in the heart of the
man), whatever the man does is good and natural
and pleasing to God. Man was made in the image
of God; it is that image that gave him his high
honor as a man and marked him out as something
unique and apart. His occupation—farmer, carpenter, miner or office worker—is altogether incidental.
Whatever he may do for his living, he is always a
man, the special creature of God.

Except for the presence of sin in human nature,
there could be no nobler sign than the one seen so

often on city streets or in the middle of busy high-
ways: "Men at Work." Whatever he may be doing,
the significant thing is that he is a man. "You made
him a little lower than the angels" (Romans 2:7).
And nothing he does can change in any degree his
essential humanity. His work can neither elevate
nor degrade him; being made in God's image, he
can elevate work by the very fact that he engages in
it. A prince walks casually across the field, and his
path becomes to the populace something different
and wonderful. A thousand oxen had walked there
before, but now the field is royal. The humble cow
path did not degrade the prince; rather, he elevated
it by his presence. That is as men see things, but it
serves to illustrate a higher truth.

"Your calling," said Meister Eckhart to the clergy
of his day, "cannot make you holy; but you can
make it holy." No matter how humble that calling
may be, a holy man can make it a holy calling. A
call to the ministry is not a call to be holy, as if the
fact of his being a minister would sanctify a man;
rather, the ministry is a calling for a holy man who
has been made holy some other way than by the
work he does. The true order is: God makes a man
holy by blood and fire and sharp discipline. Then
he calls the man to some special work, and the man
being holy makes that work holy in turn.

The anonymous author of the *Cloud of Unknowing*
sets this truth sternly before his readers: "Beware,
thou wretch . . . and hold thee never the holier nor
the better for the worthiness of thy calling . . . but
the more wretched and cursed, unless thou do that
in thee is goodly, by grace and by counsel, to live
after thy calling."

Our whole point here is that while good deeds cannot make a man good, it is likewise true that everything a good man does is good because he is a good man. Holy deeds are holy not because they are one kind of deed instead of another, but because a holy man performs them. "Every good tree bears good fruit . . . a good tree cannot bear bad fruit" (Matthew 7:18).

Every person should see to it that he is fully cleansed from all sin, entirely surrendered to the whole will of God and filled with the Holy Spirit. Then he will not be known as what he *does*, but as what he *is*. He will be a man of God first and anything else second: a man of God who paints or mines coal or farms or preaches or runs a business, but always a man of God. That and not the kind of work he does will determine the quality of his deeds.

Beauty at Christmas

FOR THOSE NATIONS of the earth which have known the story of Jesus, Christmas is undoubtedly the most beautiful time of the year.

Though the celebration of the Savior's birth occurs in the dead of winter, when in many parts of the world the streams are frozen and the landscapes cold and cheerless, still there is beauty at the Christmas season—not the tender beauty of spring flowers or the quiet loveliness of the full-blown summer, or yet the sad sweet graces of autumn colors. It is beauty of another kind, richer, deeper and more elevating, that beauty which considerations of love and mercy bring before the mind.

Though we are keenly aware of the abuses that have grown up around the holiday season, we are still not willing to surrender this ancient and loved Christmas Day to the enemy. Though those purer emotions which everyone feels at Christmas are in most hearts all too fleeting, yet it is *something* that a lost and fallen race should pay tribute, if only for a day, to those higher qualities of the mind—love and mercy and sacrifice and a life laid down for its enemies. While men are able to rise even temporarily to such heights, there is hope that they have not yet sinned away their day of grace. A heart capable of admiring and being touched by the story of the manger birth is not yet abandoned, however sinful it may be. There is yet hope in repentance.

Christmas will come and go again this year as it has done through the lost centuries and, after a brief moment of kindness felt, they of the cold, hard world will go on killing and hating and contriving to outwit and outfight each other. Things are no better, the cynics will say, no better than they were before. The whole thing is a childish myth.

We know what they think, and we know what they will say. And God knows the facts seem to give support to their ideas. But the end is not yet. The world has not seen the last of the Christ Child. That there is yet in fallen human hearts enough traces of spiritual desire to stir them to brief tribute when the chastely beautiful story of Christmas is told is sufficient answer to the cynic's charge. Men who can *want* to be good, if even for a day, can *become* good when their desire grows strong enough.

And all this is not mere theory. Thousands each year find their desire for salvation and holiness becoming too acute to bear, and turn to the One who was born in a manger to die on a cross. Then the fleeting beauty that is Christmas enters their hearts to dwell there forever. For who is it that imparts such beauty to the Christmas story? It is none other than Jesus, the Altogether Lovely.

23

The Second-best Book
for a Christian

IN ORDER TO express myself more freely on a matter that lies very near to my heart, I shall waive the rather stilted editorial *we* and speak in the first person.

The matter I have in mind is the place of the hymnbook in the devotional life of the Christian. For purposes of inward devotion, there is only one book to be placed before the hymnal, and that of course is the Bible. I say without qualification, after the Sacred Scriptures, the next best companion for the soul is a good hymnal.

For the child of God, the Bible is the book of all books, to be reverenced, loved, pored over endlessly and feasted upon as living bread and manna for the soul. It is the first-best book, the *only* indispensable book. To ignore it or neglect it is to doom our minds to error and our hearts to starvation.

After the Bible, the hymnbook is next. And remember, I do not say a songbook or a book of gospel songs, but a real hymnal containing the cream of the great Christian hymns left to us by the ages.

One of the serious weaknesses of present-day evangelicalism is the mechanical quality of its thinking. A utilitarian Christ has taken the place of the radiant Savior of other and happier times. This Christ is able to save, it is true, but He is thought to do so in a practical across-the-counter manner, paying our debt and tearing off the receipt like a court clerk acknowledging a paid-up fine. A bank-teller psychology characterizes much of the religious thinking in our little gospel circle. The tragedy of it is that it is truth without being all the truth.

If modern Christians are to approach the spiritual greatness of Bible saints or know the inward delights of the saints of post-biblical times, they must correct this imperfect view and cultivate the beauties of the Lord our God in sweet, personal experience. In achieving such a happy state, a good hymnbook will help more than any other book in the world except the Bible itself.

A great hymn embodies the purest concentrated thoughts of some lofty saint who may have long ago gone from the earth and left little or nothing behind him except that hymn. To read or sing a true hymn is to join in the act of worship with a great and gifted soul in his moments of intimate devotion. It is to hear a lover of Christ explaining to his Savior why he loves Him; it is to listen in without embarrassment on the softest whisperings of undying love between the bride and the heavenly Bridegroom.

Sometimes our hearts are strangely stubborn and will not soften or grow tender no matter how much praying we do. At such times, it is often found that the reading or singing of a good hymn will melt the ice jam and start the inward affections flowing. That is one of the uses of the hymnbook. Human emotions are curious and difficult to arouse, and there is always a danger that they may be aroused by the wrong means and for the wrong reasons.

The human heart is like an orchestra, and it is important that when the soul starts to sound its melodies, a David or a Bernard or a Watts or a Wesley should be on the podium. Constant devotion to the hymnbook will guarantee this happy event and will, conversely protect the heart from being led by evil conductors.

Every Christian should have lying beside his Bible a copy of some standard hymnbook. He should read out of one and sing out of the other, and he will be surprised and delighted to discover how much they are alike. Gifted Christian poets have in many of our great hymns set truth to music. Isaac Watts and Charles Wesley (possibly above all others) were able to marry the harp of David to the Epistles of Paul and to give us singing doctrine, ecstatic theology that delights while it enlightens.

The Vital Place of Self-criticism

A LL THINGS ELSE BEING EQUAL, a Christian will make spiritual progress exactly in proportion to his ability to criticize himself.

Paul said, "But if we judged ourselves, we would not come under judgment" (1 Corinthians 11:31). We escape the critical judgment of God by exercising critical self-judgment. It is as simple as that.

We often hear the axiom "Practice makes perfect." The fact is that practice, far from making perfect, actually confirms us in our faults unless it is carried on in a humble, self-critical spirit. The whole philosophy of instruction rests upon the idea that the learner is wrong and is seeking to be made right. No teacher can correct his pupil unless the pupil comes to him in humility. The only proper attitude for the learner is one of humble self-distrust. "I am ignorant," he says, "and am willing to be taught. I am wrong and am willing to be corrected." In this childlike spirit, the mind is made capable of improvement.

The rapidity with which improvement is made in the life will depend altogether upon the degree of self-criticism we bring to our prayers and to the school of daily living. Let a man fall under the delusion that he has arrived, and all progress is stopped until he has seen his error and forsaken it. Paul said, "Not that I have already obtained all this, or have already been made perfect, but I press on to take hold of that for which Christ Jesus took hold of me" (Philippians 3:12).

Some Christians hope in a vague kind of way that time will help them to grow better. They look to the passing of the years to mellow them and make them more Christlike. This is such a tender and pathetic thought that one hesitates to expose its essential error. But we had better know the facts now while we can do something about them rather than go on moist-eyed and dreamily hopeful—and wholly wrong. A crooked tree does not straighten with age; neither does a crooked Christian.

All this is to say that a growing Christian must have at his roots the life-giving waters of penitence. The cultivation of a penitential spirit is absolutely essential to spiritual progress. The lives of great saints teach us that self-distrust is vital to godliness. Even while the obedient soul lies prostrate before God, or goes on in reverent obedience convinced that he is carrying out the will of God with a perfect conscience, he will yet feel a sense of utter brokenness and a deep consciousness that he is still far from being what he ought to be. This is one of the many paradoxical situations in which the humble man will find himself as he follows on to know the Lord.

We have all seen the person who begins all arguments with the unassailable proposition that he is right and reasons from there. We have received a few letters which purported to settle all questions, not by bringing forth reasons, but by establishing the writer's qualifications to pronounce judgment. "How dare you question my actions," he says. "I am the foremost leader in my field. I have written this many books and spoken to this many people over a long period of this many years." Ergo, I am not to be trifled with, nor are my opinions to be questioned. If I do it, it is right. *Ispe dixit.* He has said it.

This kind of thing would be comical if it were not tragic. We mention it only to point up the truth under present consideration and to show by horrible example what long continued self-assurance will do to a human character. Let the public accept a man as unusual, and he is soon tempted to accept himself as being above reproof. Soon a hard shell of impenitence covers his heart and chokes his spiritual life almost out of existence. The cure, if there is to be a cure, would be simple, of course. Let him look to his past and to the cross where Jesus died. If he can still defend himself after that, then let him look into his own heart and tell what he finds there. If after that he can still boast, close the coffin lid.

We might point out a danger here (for there will always be perils in the way of spiritual progress): it is that we become morbidly introspective and lose the legitimate happy cheer from our souls. This we must never do, and we can avoid it by permitting Christ to engage our attention, rather than our own souls. The safe rule is, whenever we look at ourselves, be penitent; when we look at Christ, be joyous. And look at Christ most of the time, look-

ing inward only to correct our faults and grieve for
our imperfections.

God's Best Gift

GOD'S GIFTS ARE MANY; His best gift is one. It is the gift of Himself. Above all gifts, God desires most to give Himself to His people. Our nature being what it is, we are the best fitted of all creatures to know and enjoy God. "For Thou madest us for Thyself, and our heart is restless, until it repose in Thee" (from *The Confessions of St. Augustine*).

When God told Aaron, "You will have no inheritance in their land, nor will you have any share among them; I am your share and your inheritance among the Israelites," He in fact promised a portion infinitely above all the real estate in Palestine and all the earth thrown in (Numbers 18:20). To possess God—this is the inheritance ultimate and supreme.

There is a sense in which God never gives any gift except he gives Himself with it. The love of God, what is it but God giving Himself in love? The mercy of God is but God giving Himself in mercy, and so with all other blessings and benefits so freely showered upon the children of atonement. Deep within all divine blessing is the Divine One Himself dwelling as in a sanctuary.

Absalom dwelt two full years in Jerusalem and saw not the king's face, though the king was his own father. Are there not many in the kingdom of God who have no awareness of God, who seem not to know that they have the right to sit at the King's table and commune with the King? This is an evil which I have seen under the sun, and it is a hard and grievous burden.

To know God, this is eternal life; this is the purpose for which we are and were created. The destruction of our God-awareness was the master blow struck by Satan in the dark day of our transgression.

To give God back to us was the chief work of Christ in redemption. To impart Himself to us in personal experience is the first purpose of God in salvation. To bring acute God-awareness is the best help the Spirit brings in sanctification. All other steps in grace lead up to this.

Were we allowed but one request, we might gain at a stroke all things else by praying one all-embracing prayer:

> Thyself, Lord! Give me Thyself and I can want no more.

Beware Respect of Persons

THERE IS AN EVIL which I have seen under the sun—one that grows and does not diminish. And it is all the more dangerous because it is done without evil aforethought but, as it were, carelessly and without wrong intent.

It is the evil of giving to them that have and withholding from them that have not. It is the evil of blessing with a loud voice them that are already blessed and letting the unblessed and the outcast lie forgotten.

Let a man appear in a local Christian fellowship and let him be one whose fame is bruited abroad, whose presence will add something to the one who entertains him, and immediately a score of homes will be thrown open and every eager hospitality will be extended to him. But the obscure and the unknown must be content to sit on the fringes of the Christian circle and not once be invited into any home.

This is a great evil and an iniquity that awaits the judgment of the great day. And it is so widespread that scarcely any of us can claim to be free from it. So we condemn it only with utter humility and with acknowledgment that we too have been in some measure guilty.

No observant man will attempt to deny that a

vast amount of Christian money is being spent on those who do not need it, while the poor and the needy and such as have no helper must often go unnoticed and unhelped, even though they too are Christians and servants of our common Lord. (The modern church would appear to be as blind and partial as the world in this matter.)

Our Lord warned us against the snare of showing kindness only to such as could return such kindness and so cancel out any positive good we may have thought we were doing. By this test, a world of religious activity is being wasted in our churches. To invite in well-fed and well-groomed friends to share our hospitality with the full knowledge that we will be invited to receive the same kindness again on the first convenient evening is in no sense an act of Christian hospitality. It is of the earth earthy; its motive is fleshly; no sacrifice is entailed; its moral content is nil and it will be accounted wood, hay, stubble before the judgment seat of Christ.

The evil here discussed was common among the Pharisees of New Testament times. In chapter 23 of Matthew, Christ mercilessly exposed the whole thing, and in so doing earned the undying enmity of those who practiced it. The Pharisees were bad not because they entertained their friends but because they would not entertain the poor and the common among the people. One bitter accusation which they hurled against Christ was that He received sinners and ate with them. This they would not stoop to do, and in their high pride, they became seven times worse than the worst among the sinners whom they so coldly rejected.

In spite of our lip-service to democracy, Americans are a decidedly class-conscious people. The very politicians and educators and church leaders among us who sound abroad the praises of the common man and plead for equal rights for all are in private practice as aloof from the plain people as the proudest monarch could ever be. There exists among us an aristocracy composed of famous people, rich men, social lions, actors, public figures and headliners of one kind or another, and these are a class apart. Beneath them, standing off in wide-eyed admiration, are the millions of anonymous men and women who make up the mass of the population. And they have nothing in their favor—except that they were in the heart of Jesus when He died upon the cross.

Within the church also there exists a class consciousness, a reflection of that found in society. This has been brought over into the church from the world. Its spirit is completely foreign to the spirit of Christ, utterly opposed to it, indeed; and yet it determines to a large degree the conduct of Christians. This is the source of the evil we mention here.

Gospel churches which mostly begin with the lowly are usually not content till they attain some degree of wealth and social acceptance. Then they gradually fall into classes, determined largely by the wealth and education of the members. The individuals that comprise the top layer of these various classes go on to become pillars of the religious society and are soon entrenched in places of leadership and influence. It is then that their great temptation comes upon them, the temptation to cater to their own class and to neglect the poor and the ignorant that make up the swarming population around them. They soon become hardened to every appeal of the Holy Spirit toward meekness and humility. Their homes are spotless, their clothes the most expensive, their friends the most exclusive. Apart from some tremendous moral upheaval, they are beyond help. And yet they may be among the most vocal exponents of Bible Christianity and heavy givers to the cause of the church.

Let us not become indignant at this blunt portrayal of facts. Let us rather humble ourselves to serve God's poor. Let us seek to be like Jesus in our devotion to the forgotten of the earth who have nothing to recommend them but their poverty and their heart-hunger and their tears.

Religion in the Passive Voice

MOST READERS WILL remember (some with just a trace of nostalgia) his or her early struggles to learn the difference between the active and the passive voice in English grammar, and how it finally dawned that in the active voice, the subject *performs an act*; in the passive voice, the subject *is acted upon*. Thus, "I love" is active, and "I am loved" is passive.

A good example of this distinction is to be found at the nearest mortuary. There the undertaker is active and the dead are passive. One acts while the others receive the action.

Now what is normal in a mortuary may be, and in this instance is, altogether abnormal in a church. Yet we have somehow gotten ourselves into a state where almost all church religion is passive. A limited number of professionals act, and the mass of religious people are content to receive the action. The minister, like the undertaker, performs his professional service while the members of the congregation relax and passively "enjoy" the service.

One reason for this condition is the failure of the clergy to grasp the true purpose of preaching. There is a feeling that the work of the preacher is to instruct merely, whereas the real work of the preacher is to instruct *with an end to securing moral action from the hearers.* As long as there has been no moral response to the instruction, the hearers are passive merely and might as well be dead. Indeed, in one sense they are dead already.

We would make a clear distinction here between moral action and mere religious activity. In truth there is already too much of that popular type of activity which does little more than agitate the surface of religion. Its never-ending squirrel-cage motion gives the impression that much is being done, when actually nothing really important is happening and no genuine spiritual progress is being made. From such we must turn away.

By moral action, we mean a voluntary response to the Christian message: not merely the acceptance of Christ as our personal Savior but a submission to the obligation implicit in the doctrine of the Lordship of Jesus. We must free ourselves from the inadequate concept of the gospel as being only "good news," and accept the total meaning of the Christian message centering in the cross of Christ. We must restore again to the church the idea that the offer of salvation by faith in Christ carries with it the condition that there must be also a surrender of the life to God in complete obedience.

Anything less than this puts the whole thing in the passive voice. A lifetime of passive listening to the truth without responding to it paralyzes the will and causes a fatty degeneration of the heart. The purpose of Bible teaching is to secure a moral and spiritual change in the whole life. Failing this, the whole thing may be wasted.

Help from Paul's Trials

THE CHRISTIAN WHO finds himself in trouble for his faith's sake may draw a lot of consolation from Paul's epistles to the Corinthians.

Nowhere else in the entire New Testament is the humanity of the great apostle seen so clearly as when he staggers under the cruel attacks of the anti-Paul bloc in the Corinthian church. His sufferings are there the most poignant and nearest to the sufferings of Christ because they are inward and of the soul. For always the soul can suffer as the body cannot.

Paul's Corinthian detractors first tried to discredit him entirely by starting a whispering campaign to the effect that he was actually no apostle but a power-hungry impostor seeking to bring them under his control. When the apostle had written his reply in defense of his apostolic authority, they then shifted their attack and accused him of other kinds of double dealing. "He gives himself as a reference for himself," they said sarcastically. "He must have letters of recommendation like a common traveling preacher. Such a man cannot be an apostle." Paul had to answer that, and he did. But it was not easy. His second epistle to the Corinthians was surely one of the most difficult he was ever called upon to write, for he was forced for the church's sake to speak in his own defense. His beloved fellow Christians must trust him if he is to help them, so he will state his case frankly, even if his whole soul shrinks from the task. The words "I am speaking as a fool," "I am become a fool," indicate how deeply he felt the humiliation. But he sacrificed himself for the good of the church and let his enemies think what they would. That was Paul's way.

In reading Second Corinthians, it is difficult to restrain a feeling of real pity for the noble old man as he sweats under the bitter lashings of the enemy. But such pity is wasted now. He has long been where the wicked cease from troubling and the toil-worn are at rest. For many long years, his eyes have gazed upon the vision beautific in the land where

> The red rose of Sharon
> Distills its heartsome bloom
> And fills the air of heaven
> With ravishing perfume.

He walks now with the noble army of martyrs and shares the goodly fellowship of the prophets and the glorious company of the apostles. He does not need our pity.

But from Paul and his afflictions we may learn much truth, some of it depressing and some altogether elevating and wonderful. We may learn, for instance, that malice needs nothing to live on; it can feed on itself. A contentious spirit will find something to quarrel about. A faultfinder will find occasion to accuse a Christian even if his life is as chaste as an icicle and pure as snow. A man of ill will does not hesitate to attack, even if the object of his hatred be a prophet or the very Son of God Himself. If John comes fasting, he says he has a devil; if Christ comes eating and drinking, he says He is a winebibber and a glutton. Good men are made to appear evil by the simple trick of dredging up from his own heart the evil that is there and attributing it to them.

But Paul's trials yield for us more than this negative kind of blessing. They also teach us positive lessons to help us to endure affliction by that well-known psychological law by which we are able to identify ourselves with others and "halve our griefs while we double our joys." It is always easier to bear what we know someone has borne successfully before us.

From the trials and triumphs of Paul, we gather, too, that happiness is really not indispensable to a Christian. There are many ills worse than heartaches. It is scarcely too much to say that prolonged happiness may actually weaken us, especially if we *insist* upon being happy as the Jews insisted upon flesh in the wilderness. In so doing, we may try to avoid those spiritual responsibilities which would in the nature of them bring a certain measure of heaviness and affliction to the soul.

The best thing is neither to seek nor seek to avoid troubles but to follow Christ and take the bitter with the sweet as it may come. Whether we are happy or unhappy at any given time is not important. That we be in the will of God is all that matters. We may safely leave with Him the incident of heartache or happiness. He will know how much we need of either or both.

The Unchanging World
of Men

THERE IS A WELL-KNOWN saying which I think originated with the French, that the more things change the more they remain the same.

The wisdom of this saying may be seen in almost every department of human life, the reason probably being that of all the things that change and still remain unchanged, there is no better example than human nature itself.

And when do we see the unchanging quality of human nature more perfectly than at Christmastime? Consider the radical difference between today's world and the world into which the Baby Jesus was born. Compared with our 20th-century civilization, everything surrounding the wondrous Child was crude and primitive. Jesus was born in a stable, not in a hospital; His mother was attended by a midwife, not by a skilled scientist; His baby face was lighted by a tallow candle, not by an electric bulb; He traveled into Egypt on the back of the lowly burro, not by auto or streamlined train.

While Jesus grew through the various stages of developing childhood, He never saw a mechanical device more complicated than a cart. He never saw paper, or plastic, or a telephone, or a radio, or a camera, or a printed sheet, or a paved highway, or a gun, or a steam engine, or an electric motor. No one in His day ever got vaccinated or took vitamin pills or consulted a psychiatrist or had a song recorded or rode in a balloon or airplane or elevator. The people of His time had to get along without floating soap, chlorophyl toothpaste, rubber gloves, ready-mix flour, canned peas, Alka-seltzer, parking meters, Wheaties, puffed rice, electric razors, in-a-door beds, wristwatches, typewriters and Band-aids. Jesus never nursed from a rubber nipple or ate a scientifically compounded formula or played with an "educational" toy or attended a progressive school or saw a comic book or owned a toy bomb shelter.

Judged against our present highly complicated manner of life, the people of Palestine in the days of Christ's flesh scarcely lived at all. Were we forced suddenly to live as they did, we would feel that the bottom had dropped out of the world. Surely people who lived so close to nature could not be "real people" (to borrow the language of the liberals).

But they were real human beings all right, those simple people of Bethlehem and Capernaum. And the striking thing is that they were *exactly* the kind of people we are. Not one minor variation distinguishes them from us. Only the externals were different. Those things that have changed belong to the outer man; the inner man has not changed in the slightest.

We of the 20th century have exactly the same basic needs as the people of the first century. We feel the weight of sin and mortality just as they did.

We long for peace and life eternal exactly as they did. We are tortured by fears, stunned by losses, grieved by betrayals, hurt by enmities, made heartsick by failures, scared by threatening death, chased by the devil and frightened cold by the thought of coming judgment. They sat in their simple houses and worried by candlelight. We speed along in sleek, shiny cars and do our worrying between stoplights. But the end result is the same for everybody: slow progress backward toward old age and the grave with no place to hide and no friend to help.

God called His Son's name *Jesus* because He knew the human race needed deliverance from sin; and He sent the angels to announce "Peace on earth" because He knew the world needed deliverance from the gnawing tooth of inward fear. And nothing basic has changed. We today need Jesus, and we need Him for the same reasons they needed Him 2,000 years ago. The more things change, the more they remain the same.

Meditation on the New Year

IT WAS JOHN MILTON who said that hope springs eternal in the human breast. Indeed hope is such a vital thing that were it to die out of the heart of mankind, the burden of life could not long be sustained.

But precious as this hope may be, it is yet, when it is ill-founded, a dangerous thing. The hope, for instance, which almost all people feel, of long life here on earth, can be for many a deadly snare, a fatal delusion. The average man, when he thinks of his future, suspends reason, falls back on unreasoning hope and creates for himself an expectation of peaceful and unnumbered days yet to come. This blind optimism works all right till the last day, that inevitable last day which comes to all; then it betrays its victim into the pit from which there is no escape.

The perils of groundless hope threaten the Christian too. James sharply rebuked the believers of his day for presumptuously assuming an earthly future they had no real assurance would be theirs,

> Now listen, you who say, "Today or tomorrow we will go to this or that city, spend a year there, carry on business and make money."

Why, you do not even know what will happen tomorrow. What is your life? You are a mist that appears for a little while and then vanishes. Instead, you ought to say, "If it is the Lord's will, we will live and do this or that." As it is, you boast and brag. All such boasting is evil. (James 4:13–16)

Would it not be good for us to put away the vain dream of countless earthly days and face up to the blunt fact that our days on earth may actually not be many?

For the true church, there is always the possibility that Christ may return. Some good and serious souls hold this to be more than a possibility, for it seems to them as it seems to this writer that "the earth is grown old and the judgment is near," and the voices of the holy prophets are sounding in our ears.

And when He comes, there will not be a moment's notice, not an added day or hour in which to make frantic last-minute preparations.

Be careful, or your hearts will be weighed down with dissipation, drunkenness and the anxieties of life, and that day will close on you unexpectedly like a trap. For it will come upon all those who live on the face of the whole earth. Be always on the watch, and pray that you may be able to escape all that is about to happen, and that you may be able to stand before the Son of Man. (Luke 21:34–36)

Altogether apart from the prophetic expectations of devout men, there is the familiar fact of death itself. Of those Christians who had died, Paul said simply, "Some have fallen asleep." What a vast and goodly company they make, those sleeping saints, and how their number will be increased this year. And which ones among us can give assurance that he may not join them before all the days of the year have run their course?

Since we know not what a day may bring forth, does it not appear to be the part of wisdom to live each day as if it were to be the last? Any preparation we will wish we had made, let us make it now. Anything we will wish we had done, let us do it today. Any gift we will wish we had made, let us make it while time is on our side.

At the great unveiling, there will be other emotions beside joy. There will be grief and shock and self-reproach and disillusionment. But it need not be so for you and me if we will but use the information we have at hand, if we will but take advantage of the opportunities that lie beside our pathway and the promises that jut like uncut diamonds from the Sacred Scripture. Yesterday may have been marked by shameful failure, prayerlessness, backsliding. Today all that can be changed and tomorrow—if there is for us an earthly tomorrow—can be filled with purity and power and radiant, fruitful service.

The big thing is to be sure we are not lulled to sleep by a false hope, that we do not waste our time dreaming about days that are not to be ours. The main thing is to make *today* serve us by getting ready for any possible tomorrow. Then whether we live or die, whether we toil on in the shadow or rise to meet the returning Christ, all will be well.

CHAPTER

31

The Witness of the Spirit:
What Is It?

SOMEONE WROTE TO ME recently asking what I
meant by a statement which occurs in the book-
let *Paths to Power*, which I wrote some years ago.
The passage reads: "No one was ever filled with
the Holy Spirit without knowing it. The Holy Spirit
always announces Himself to the human consciousness." What bothered my correspondent was
the nature of this "announcement." Of what does it
consist? How may we recognize it? Is it some kind
of physical evidence, or what?

This whole question is worthy of larger treatment
than I can give it in this limited space. But possibly
these thoughts will prove helpful to any who may
be confused about the nature of spiritual evidence.

There is such a thing as the secret workings of the
Spirit in the soul of man, for a time unknown and
unsuspected by the individual. In fact, most of the
fruits of the Spirit are unsuspected by the man in
whom they are found. The most loving, most patient, most compassionate soul is unlikely to be
aware of these graces. He is almost certain to believe that he is anything but loving or patient or
kind. Others will discover the operations of the

Spirit within him long before he will and will thank God for his sweet Christian character while he may at the same time be walking in great humility before God, mourning the absence of the very graces that others know he possesses.

Then, there is another kind of divine working that may occur without our being aware of it, or at least without our recognizing it for what it is. This is that wondrous operation of God known in theology as *prevenient grace*. It may be simple "conviction," or a strange longing which nothing can satisfy, or a powerful aspiration after eternal values, or a feeling of disgust for sin and a desire to be delivered from its repulsive coils. These strange workings within are the stirrings of the Holy Spirit but are rarely identified as such by the soul that is undergoing the experience.

But there are two acts of God within the life of the seeking man that are never done without his knowlege. One is the miracle of the new birth and the other is the anointing of the Holy Spirit.

Of the new birth, Paul explicitly states, "The Spirit himself testifies with our spirit, that we are God's children" (Romans 8:16), and John says, "Anyone who believes in the Son of God has this testimony in his heart" (1 John 5:10). These passages declare the *fact* of a divine witness but do not state the *nature* of it. This has made it possible for various people to read into it their own peculiar psychological reactions and set up those reactions as criteria by which they judge the spiritual claims of everyone. Some at the time of their conversion have felt unusually light on their feet; others have heard voices or seen lights or felt an unseen hand pass over them. In some places, the new convert must shout aloud or his profession is not accepted.

Again, the experience of the Spirit's fullness coming upon the believer's heart is often judged by the amount and quality of emotional charge that accompanies it. Some go so far as to declare bluntly that no one is filled with the Spirit who has not experienced certain physical phenomena, particularly the act of speaking in unidentified tongues. Others will settle for an increased degree of joy or more effectiveness in their service.

All this is wrong, both scripturally and psychologically. It is the result of a misunderstanding of the nature of man's soul and of the relation of the spirit of man to the Spirit of God.

The workings of God in the hearts of redeemed men always overflow into observable conduct. Certain moral changes will take place immediately in the life of the new convert. A moral revolution without will accompany the spiritual revolution that has occurred within. As the evangelists tell us, even the cat will know it when the head of the house is converted. And the grocer will know it too, and the old cronies in the haunts where the man used to hang out will suspect that something has happened when they miss the new Christian from his accustomed place. All this is collateral proof of the validity of the man's Christian profession. *But it is in no sense evidence to the man's own heart. It is not the witness of the Spirit.*

The witness of the Spirit is a sacred inner thing which cannot be explained. It is altogether personal and cannot be passed from one to another. Deep calleth unto deep at the noise of God's waterspouts, and the outward ear cannot hear what it says. Much less can the worldly onlooker know what is taking place. The Spirit whispers its mysterious Presence to the heart, and the heart knows without knowing *how* it knows. Just as we know we are alive by unmediated knowledge and without recourse to proof, so we know we are alive in the Holy Spirit. Our knowledge is by immediate cognition altogether independent of inference and without the support of reason. The witness is in the hidden regions of the spirit, too deep for proof, where external evidence is invalid and "signs" are of no use.

When all is said, it may easily be that the great difference between professing Christians (the *important* difference in this day) is not between modernists and evangelicals but between those who have reduced Christianity to an intellectual formula and those who believe that the true essence of our faith lies in the supernatural workings of the Spirit in a region of the soul not accessible to mere reason.

32

Eloquence Can Bring a Snare

THERE ARE FEW THINGS in religious circles held in greater esteem than eloquence. Yet there are few things of less actual value or that bring with them greater temptation or more harm.

One qualification everyone expects a preacher to have is the ability to discourse fluently on almost any religious or moral subject. Yet such ability is at best a doubtful asset and unless brought to Christ for cleansing may easily turn out to be the greatest enemy the preacher faces here below. The man who finds that he is able to preach on a moment's notice should accept his ability as an obstacle over which he must try to get victory before he is at his best for God and His kingdom.

Moses was not a fluent man. His words spoken to God must be accepted as being a sincere and fair appraisal of the facts: "O Lord, I have never been eloquent, neither in the past nor since you have spoken to your servant. I am slow of speech and tongue" (Exodus 4:10). The Lord did not try to cheer up His doubting servant by telling him that he had misjudged his ability. He allowed Moses' statement to stand unchallenged. But He said to

Moses, "What about your brother Aaron the Levite? I know he can speak well." God gave Aaron an "A" in speech. He was undoubtedly an eloquent man. Yet it was the halting Moses, not the fluent Aaron, who faced Pharaoh time after time in defense of Israel; it was Moses, not the eloquent Aaron, who wrote the brilliant and beautiful story of the creation; it was Moses who penned the Book of Deuteronomy, one of the most poetical and moving books ever written. Was Aaron too fluent for God to use after all? I do not claim to know why, but whatever the reason, we have but few samples of Aaron's words in the Bible and countless pages of Moses'.

The reason back of all this is that great emotions rarely produce fluency of speech, whereas shallow feelings are sure to express themselves in many words. We tend to use words in inverse proportion to the depth of our feelings. Some of the profoundest emotions of the heart utter themselves in a chaste brevity of words, as when John tells us of Christ's sharp grief at the grave of Lazarus. He says simply, "Jesus wept." With exquisite good taste, the scholars who divided the Bible into verses allowed those two words to stand alone. Nothing more is needed to reveal the mighty depth of Christ's love for His friend.

Again, that world-shaking event, the crucifixion of Christ, is stated in four words, "There they crucified him." One shudders to think what fanfare and buildup such a stupendous event would require if written by the shallow novelists or dramatists of our day. To represent such a solemn event on the stage would cost thousands of dollars and would require enough words to fill a dozen pages of script. The reason for the difference is of course that the evangelists *felt* the crucifixion and instinctively spoke of it in few words.

To follow this thought further, it is only necessary to note the simple brevity of the announcement of our Lord's resurrection. The "young man" told the inquiring disciples the story in three words: "He is risen." These needed no eloquent preface to such a wondrous announcement. Where there have been mighty deeds, there need be no multitude of words to tell of them. Many words are required only where the deeds have been too feeble to speak for themselves.

Most religious people have been guilty of multiplying words as substitutes for worthy deeds, and of all such the writer of these lines is probably the worst offender. But because we have offended is not sufficient reason for our going on to repeat the offense. It is better that we face the whole thing with self-effacing humility and try to correct our fault.

It remains only to be said that where shallow eloquence is most out of place and where it is oftenest found is the prayer meeting. The most halting speaker seems to become unusually fluent when he kneels to pray, especially when he has an audience. I have heard much flowery speech in the prayer room, and I suppose I have uttered a good deal of it. But again, there is no reason for continuing to utter words without wisdom. A conscious sense of the presence of God is a wonderful cure for empty talk, whether in the pulpit or in the pew.

When the Holy Spirit falls on a man, he is likely

to become strangely eloquent. Out of the awe and silence of the soul comes an uprushing of power-filled words that move the hearts of the hearers to tears and to action. Such eloquence as this is something else; of this we do not here speak. Of this latter we need a great deal more, but we can do with a lot fewer empty words in religious circles.

Religion of the Intellect versus Religion of the Spirit

THERE IS A DEEPLY spiritual and thoroughly mystical quality in New Testament religion that we cannot afford to ignore if we would be Christians in fact as well as in name.

I think it well to let our worshiping hearts decide our theological questions. After the purity of the text has been established and the mind assured that the translation is trustworthy, the best source of true light is always the Spirit-illuminated heart. A praying heart, aglow with love for God, will intuit truth, will pass behind the veil and see and hear that which is not lawful to be uttered, which indeed cannot be uttered or even intellectually understood.

It is my opinion that the real battle line in the theological war today is not the line that separates fundamentalism from liberalism. That war has been fought and won. No one need be in any wise confused on the question of Bible theology versus man-conceived liberalism. Both sides have said their say boldly. Everyone can know where he stands on such matters as the inspiration of the Scriptures, the deity of Jesus Christ, salvation through the blood of atonement, death and judgment, heaven and hell. The true battle line is elsewhere.

Always the decisive conflict in religion will be where important concepts are joined in opposition, concepts so vital that they are capable of saving or wrecking the Christian faith in any given generation. At this critical juncture in church history, the real conflict is between those who hold to an objective Christianity capable of being grasped in its entirety by the human intellect and those who believe that there are far-in areas of religious experience so highly spiritual, so removed from and exalted above mere reason, that it takes a special anointing of the Holy Spirit to make them understood by the human heart. The difference is not academic merely. Should the advocates of religious intellectualism succeed in setting the direction for the church in this generation, the next generation of Christians will become helpless victims of dead orthodoxy.

In conversation with one of the better-known devotees of neo-intellectualism in evangelical circles, I asked the question bluntly, "Do you actually believe that everything essential in the Christian faith may be grasped by the human intellect?" The answer was immediate—"If I did not, I would be on my way toward agnosticism." I did not say, but might properly have said, "And if you do, you are on your way toward rationalism." For such indeed is the truth.

One of the heaviest problems the inquiring

Christian faces today is why so many good and apparently sincere religious leaders are going so far astray from the plain teachings and practices of the New Testament. Destructive elements are being innocently introduced into present-day worship and service by Bible-loving evangelicals, elements so opposed to the true genius of Christianity that the two are mutually exclusive. One or the other must go. Either these new parasitic growths must be destroyed, or they will in a short time destroy the Christian faith. Yet these deadly things are encouraged in the churches by some of the most zealous orthodox leaders. Why?

The answer is simpler than we might suppose. These leaders are depending on their brain to guide them in their religious practices. Then conceive the truth to be a doctrinal deposit, a kind of a theological road map to lead them to heaven. They check the map to make sure they are going the right direction, and after that they are on their own. No Unseen Guide is necessary. If they should be attacked by doubts, they need only stop under a lamppost and reassure themselves that they have indeed "accepted" Christ. Then they get underway again with complete confidence that they are on the same road as the apostles and prophets.

The question being discussed by many these days—why religion is increasing and morality slipping, all at the same time—finds its answer in this very error, the error of religious intellectualism. Men have a form of godliness but deny the power thereof. The text alone will not elevate the moral life. To become morally effective, the truth must be accompanied by a mystic element, the very element supplied by the Spirit of truth. The Holy Spirit will not be banished to a footnote without taking terrible vengeance against His banishers. That vengeance may be seen today in the nervous, giggling, worldly minded and thoroughly carnal fundamentalism that is spreading over the land. Doctrinally, it wears the robes of scriptural belief, but beyond that it resembles the religion of Christ and His apostles not at all.

The mysterious presence of the Spirit is vitally necessary if we are to avoid the pitfalls of religion. As the fiery pillar led Israel through the wilderness, so the Spirit of truth must lead us all our journey through. One text alone could improve things mightily for us if we would but obey it: "Trust in the Lord with all your heart and lean not on your own understanding" (Proverbs 3:5).

Does Our Lord Pray for the Unsaved?

CHRIST IN HIS HIGH-PRIESTLY prayer specifically states, "I am not praying for the world, but for those you have given me" (John 17:9). That is what He said; it only remains to learn by reverent comparison with other Scripture just what the words mean.

To insist that by these words Christ meant that He *never* prayed for sinners would be to read into the words more than is there. We must remember that these words were spoken in a particular context; the great High Priest was appearing before the throne of mercy as Advocate and Intercessor and could at that time include in His prayers only those who were His own.

When a high priest of the Old Testament appeared before the mercy seat to offer blood for the sins of Israel, his intercessions extended to Israel only. They were the only ones for whom that atonement was made. They were the only ones who trusted in Him and looked to Him for help. Christ came in fulfillment of the Old Testament type, and it may safely be assumed that the prayer of John 17 was made only for those who accept Christ's atonement and avail themselves of the protection it affords.

Two other considerations may help us here. One is that our Lord *did* on at least one occasion pray for sinners. "Father, forgive them, for they do not know what they are doing," was a request made to God on behalf of evil men. Is it not reasonable that if Christ prayed for sinners once, He may be expected to pray for them again? Also we must remember that Jesus was a Son of man and frequently referred to Himself by that title. As such, He had and has a relationship to the whole human race. Is it thinkable that He would not pray for the race to which He belonged?

I realize that we are on holy ground right here, and common modesty would urge us to withhold any dogmatic judgments. But I believe that the question, Does our Lord pray for the unsaved? may be answered truthfully as follows: (1) As High Priest of His own redeemed people, Christ prays an efficacious prayer of intercession which avails only for those who trust Him as their Redeemer and Lord. This prayer is found in essence in John 17. (2) As Son of man and Savior, He prays for the lost world as well. Unless His prayers for the world were ascending to heaven, the judgment of God would not be withheld for a moment from the earth.

Why Do We Love Facts and Despise Truth?

O NE OF THE GREAT religious thinkers of this century has pointed out a strange contradiction in the mental attitude of our times—our eager love of knowledge and our universal neglect of truth.

That men love knowledge is too well demonstrated to need proof, if by knowledge we mean facts, know-how, statistics, technical information, scientific and mechanical skills. Our printing presses are constantly rolling out books crammed with useful information. Our schools are bulging with eager students bent on acquiring all possible knowledge in the shortest possible time. Among the most popular and lucrative radio programs on the air today are those designed to discover how many unrelated bits of information the participants possess. "Who? What? When? Where?" run the endless questions, and the impression is created that the one who can answer the greatest number is in some way a superior person.

It is vitally important that we make a sharp distinction between knowledge and truth—that is, between the knowledge that is but the sum of facts we possess and truth which is a moral and spiritual thing. It is possible to fill the mind with facts and be none the better for it, for facts have no moral or spiritual significance. Facts bear the same relation to truth that a corpse bears to a man. They serve as a medium whereby truth relates itself to outward life and circumstance but must depend for their significance upon the inner essence of truth.

The Christian is concerned primarily with truth, and especially with Him who is Truth incarnated. Facts are not to be despised. They are to be sought for their practical value and used in the service of truth, but they are never to be allowed to substitute for those "treasures of wisdom and knowledge" which are hidden in Christ.

In this day of moral confusion, truth is not always understood to be a master to which we must render obedience; it is rather conceived to be a servant which we may use to further ends that lie outside of truth. Private ends are often sought by the aid of truth, ends that stand outside of and bear no relation whatever to truth itself.

If we were to observe strict accuracy, we should always capitalize the word Truth, for when we have pushed it back as far as we can, we will come to God Himself. For this reason, truth will always be the master, never the servant. And truth can never be understood apart from its moral and spiritual implications.

36

Our Brother, Peter

FOR SOME QUEER REASON, we seem to love people more when they are not too perfect.

In the presence of a faultless saint, the average one of us feels ill at ease. We are likely to be discouraged rather than inspired by the sight of a character too impeccable to be human. We draw more help from a man if we know that he is going through the fire along with the rest of us, and we may even take courage from the fact that he does not enjoy it any more than we do.

This may be the reason Christians have always felt a special affection for Simon Peter. We speak of Paul with solemn respect but of Peter with an understanding smile. When the doughty old fisherman is mentioned, the face of the ordinary struggling Christian lights up. Here is a man who is one of us, we say to ourselves. He had faults, but he conquered them and went on to become great in spite of them. He was no alabaster saint, faintly redolent of incense, gazing absently over our heads as we labor onward through the storm. He too knew the sting of the wind and the fury of the waves, and what is more to our comfort, he did not always acquit himself like a hero when he was in a tight spot. And that helps a lot when we are not doing too well ourselves.

Peter contained or has been accidentally associated with more contradictions than almost any other Bible character. He appeared to be a combination of courage and cowardice, reverence and disrespect, selfless devotion and dangerous self-love. Only Peter could solemnly swear that he would never desert Christ and then turn around and deny Him the first time he got in a tight place. Only Peter could fall at Jesus' feet and acknowledge his own sinfulness and then rebuke his Lord for suggesting something with which he did not agree. The two natures that strove within him made him say and do things that appeared to be in direct contradiction to each other—and all within a matter of hours. Peter was a "rock," yet he wavered, and so, I suppose, managed to become the only wavering rock in history. And he surely was the only man in the world who had faith enough to walk on water but not enough faith to continue to do so when the wind blew.

For better or for worse, that was Peter, and it took God a long time to unify his nature so that the strife within him ceased. And he had to learn some things the hard way even after Pentecost.

By a kind of poetic justice, Peter has been the center of a number of historical contradictions, or perhaps we should say traditional, for many of them lack the dignity of authentic history. They are the fabrications of the Roman special pleaders who will make a case for themselves even if they must assassinate truth to do it.

Peter is, for instance, the only man in the world

who was never married and yet had a mother-in-law; for the Bible says Peter's wife's mother lay sick of a fever, and Rome says he was not married. He was, according to legend, the first pope, yet Paul crowded him out of first place and eclipsed him easily. That first pope took a position of meek deference before Paul, a position so definitely below him that one wonders how things got that way. If Peter was pope and not Paul, why did the great official pronouncements issue from Paul and not from Peter? It is all very confusing, but not much more so than Peter himself.

Well, the good old man of God cannot be blamed for the position Rome has given him. He was long gone from the hustle and bustle of the world before anyone thought of making him a lifelong bachelor and the vicegerent of Christ on earth. Such doubtful honors he shares with Mary the mother of Christ, who in her simple modesty would be shocked speechless if she could know what manufactured glories are being accorded her now by purblind leaders of the blind.

For all his faults, or perhaps because of them, Peter could do one thing superbly: he could shed tears of grief when he had offended his Savior. The ability to repent is a sweet treasure, and one that is rare among us these days. If we had Peter's penitent heart, we might go on to have his purity and his power. Should the contemplation of Peter's faults give aid and comfort to an impenitent heart, then that heart has only itself to blame. God never intended that we should hide our unconfessed sins behind the confessed faults of a saint. Peter's contrary nature drove him to God. Unless ours does the same, Peter will have lived in vain for us.

Anyway, we are glad Peter lived, and we are glad Christ found him. He is so much like so many of us, at least in his weaknesses. It only remains for us to learn also the secret of his strength.

Beware Inflation!

T HE BIBLE WARNS against inflation, only it says it another way; it calls it being "puffed up."

There are two ways to increase size: one is to grow normally, the other to become artificially distended. The first indicates health, the second, disease. The well-fed child grows larger each year; only the abdomen of the tiny famine victim grows, and that by a pathological distention that tells of approaching death.

In the realm of the spiritual, there is real danger that we may mistake unhealthy bloat for true growth. Paul dealt frankly with this danger and pointed out that being puffed up and being built up are two different things.

We all know how prone we are to find what we are looking for in the Scriptures and in our own lives. When appraising ourselves, we sometimes unconsciously adopt the technique of the defense attorney, that of playing up everything favorable to us and conversely playing down whatever would put us in an unfavorable light. While considering my own ministry, I have often caught myself magnifying every small victory out of all fair proportion and at the same time alibiing my failures and weaknesses. It is the old trick of seeing what we want to see and closing our eyes to the things we would rather forget. This is inflation, and unless it is judged and forsaken, it can result in a completely false estimate of our life and work.

We may need to look closely to discover the relation between inflation and unbelief, but such a relation does nevertheless exist. The man of faith is so sure of his position before God that he can quietly allow himself to be overlooked, discredited, deflated, without a tremor of anxiety. He is willing to wait out God's own good time and let the wisdom of the future judgment reveal his true size and worth. The man of unbelief dare not do this. He is so unsure of himself that he demands immediate and visible proof of his success. His deep unbelief must have the support of present judgment. He looks eagerly for evidence to assure him that he is indeed somebody. And of course this hunger for present approval throws him open to the temptation to inflate his work for the sake of appearances.

This need for external support for our sagging faith accounts for the introduction into religious activities of that welter of shoddy claptrap that has become the characteristic mark of modern Christianity. The church and the minister must make a showing, and nothing would seem to be ruled out that will add to the illusion of success. At the root of this is plain unbelief. Religious people are simply not willing to wait till the Lord comes to receive their reward. They demand it now, and they get it, a circumstance over which they will shed bitter tears in the day of Christ.

To guarantee immunity to this disease of the heart, we must cultivate a spirit of faith and humility. This works as an antibody to destroy the moral bacteria that cause bloat and distention.

If we have faith, we will be concerned only with what God thinks of us. We can smile off man's opinion, whether it be favorable or unfavorable, and go our God-appointed way in complete confidence. The excited devotees of the twin gods Publicity and Reputation will race past us with no more than a pitying glance. The self-acknowledged Great of the kingdom, the Eminent, the Outstanding will ignore us or patronize us or perhaps seek to cultivate us for their ends. We in the meantime will step neither to the right hand nor to the left. We will honor all men, be courteous to everyone, love our Christian brothers, glorify God and fear nobody.

It takes a lot of courage and independence of mind to insist upon being just what we are, and no more. But when the Lord comes, we will not have cause to regret that we did.

Could This Be Our Most Critical Need?

WHEN VIEWING THE RELIGIOUS scene today, we are tempted to fix on one or another weakness and say, "This is what is wrong with the church. If this were corrected, we could recapture the glory of the early church and have pentecostal times back with us again."

This tendency to oversimplification is itself a weakness and should be guarded against always, especially when dealing with anything as complex as religion as it occurs in modern times. It takes a very young man to reduce all our present woes to a single disease and cure the whole thing with one simple remedy. Older and wiser heads will be more cautious, having learned that the prescribed nostrum seldom works for the reason that the diagnosis has not been correct. Nothing is that simple. Few spiritual diseases occur alone. Almost all are complicated by the presence of others and are so vitally interrelated as they spread over the whole religious body that it would take the wisdom of a Solomon to find a single cure.

For this reason, I am hesitant to point to any one defect in present-day Christianity and make all our troubles to stem from it alone. That so-called Bible religion in our times is suffering rapid decline is so evident as to need no proof, but just what has brought about this decline is not so easy to discover. I can only say that I have observed one significant lack among evangelical Christians which might turn out to be the real cause of most of our spiritual troubles. Of course, if that were true, then the supplying of that lack would be our most critical need.

The great deficiency to which I refer is the lack of spiritual discernment, especially among our leaders. How there can be so much Bible knowledge and so little insight, so little moral penetration, is one of the enigmas of the religious world today. I think it is altogether accurate to say that there has never before been a time in the history of the church when so many people were engaged in Bible study as are so engaged today. If the knowledge of Bible doctrine were any guarantee of godliness, this would without doubt be known in history as the age of sanctity. Instead, it may well be known as the age of the church's Babylonish captivity, or the age of worldliness, when the professed Bride of Christ allowed herself to be successfully courted by the fallen sons of men in unbelievable numbers. The body of evangelical believers, under evil influences, has during the last 25 years gone over to the world in complete and abject surrender, avoiding only a few of the grosser sins such as drunkenness and sexual promiscuity.

That this disgraceful betrayal has taken place in broad daylight with full consent of our Bible teachers and evangelists is one of the most terrible affairs in the spiritual history of the world. Yet I for one cannot believe that the great surrender was negotiated by men of evil heart who set out deliberately to destroy the faith of our fathers. Many good and clean-living people have collaborated with the quislings who betrayed us. Why? The answer can only be, *from lack of spiritual vision.* Something like a mist has settled over the church as "the shroud that enfolds all peoples, the sheet that covers all nations" (Isaiah 25:7). Such a veil once descended upon Israel: "For their minds were made dull, for to this day the same veil remains when the old covenant is read. It has not been removed, because only in Christ is it taken away. Even to this day when Moses is read, a veil covers their hearts" (2 Corinthians 3:14–15). That was Israel's tragic hour. God raised up the church and temporarily disfranchised His ancient people. He could not trust His work to blind men.

Surely we need a baptism of clear seeing if we are to escape the fate of Israel (and of every other religious body in history that forsook God). If not the greatest need, then surely one of the greatest is for the appearance of Christian leaders with prophetic vision. We desperately need seers who can see through the mist. Unless they come soon, it will be too late for this generation. And if they do come, we will no doubt crucify a few of them in the name of our worldly orthodoxy. But the cross is always the harbinger of the resurrection.

Mere evangelism is not our present need. Evangelism does no more than extend religion, of whatever kind it may be. It gains acceptance for religion among larger numbers of people without giving much thought to the *quality* of that religion. The tragedy is that present-day evangelism accepts the degenerate form of Christianity now current as the very religion of the apostles and busies itself with making converts to it with no questions asked. And all the time we are moving farther and farther from the New Testament pattern.

We must have a new reformation. There must come a violent break with that irresponsible, amusement-mad, paganized pseudo-religion which passes today for the faith of Christ and which is being spread all over the world by unspiritual men employing unscriptural methods to achieve their ends.

When the Roman church apostasized, God brought about the Reformation. When the Reformation declined, God raised up the Moravians and the Wesleys. When these movements began to die, God raised up fundamentalism and the "deeper life" groups.

Now that these have almost without exception sold out to the world—what next?